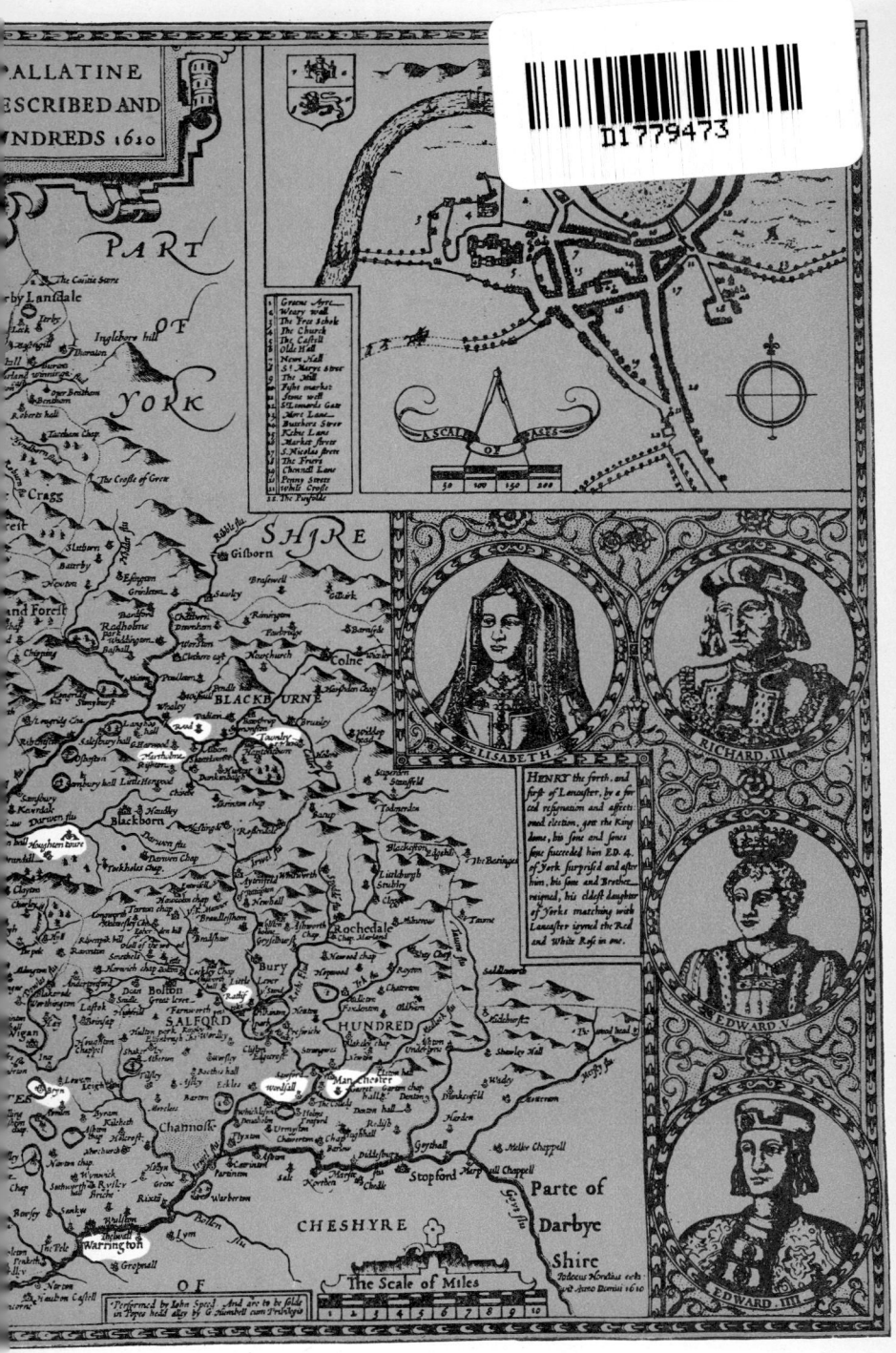

THE ANNOTATOR

THE GRAFTON PORTRAIT

The Annotator

*The Pursuit of an Elizabethan Reader of
Halle's Chronicle
Involving some Surmises
About the Early Life of
William Shakespeare*

By
ALAN KEEN
&
ROGER LUBBOCK

*With Genealogical Tables by
Norman Long-Brown &
Frances Keen*

PUTNAM
GREAT RUSSELL STREET
LONDON MCMLIV

FIRST PUBLISHED 1954

*Printed in Great Britain by
Robert Cunningham and Sons, Ltd., Alva*

CONTENTS

CHAPTER I
1940 – *a chance copy of Halle's* Chronicle – *The marginal notes – The press-mark – British Museum certification – Two Richard Newports*   1

CHAPTER II
Character of the annotator, 'A.' Young, assiduous, patriotic, methodical, Catholic – Catch-phrases – Historical interest – Similarity of interests to Shakespeare's   7

CHAPTER III
Shakespearian parallels – Verbal coincidences – Shakespeare's use of Halle – A.'s use of Shakespearian words not in Halle   20

CHAPTER IV
The 'other' Newport – Shropshire connections – Houghton – Hesketh – The Houghton will – Elizabethan players – Private companies – Strange's Men   31

CHAPTER V
The quest for Shakeshafte – Lea Hall – Sir T. Hesketh – Two indications of his players   43

CHAPTER VI
Lancashire connexions with Shakespeare – The Rufford tradition – Thomas Savage – Edward Alleyn – John Weever – A Lancashire performance of Richard III *– The Prescot playhouse – Robert Tofte – An early performance of* L.L.L. *– William Stanley – Richard Lloyd – The Nine Worthies*   49

CONTENTS

CHAPTER VII
Further Lancashire clues – Margaret Radcliffe – Early performance of Titus Andronicus, *and inclusion of a Lancashire legend – The archery scene and the Lathom screen – John Salisbury's visit to Knowsley – Hamlet Holcroft*   61

CHAPTER VIII
Shakeshafte-Shakespeare hypothesis – The name – John Shakespeare's recusancy – The young Shakespeare – "killing the calf" – Rufford – Greene and the Stanleys – The Stanleys in Shakespeare's early Histories – The Hesketh plot – Catholic support for William Stanley   74

CHAPTER IX
The track of the book – A.'s spelling – Shakespeare in Shropshire – The pressmark – Robert Worsley   88

CHAPTER X
Douay – Roman Catholic allusions in Shakespeare's plays – Robert Dibdale – Richard Houghton's voyage – Shakespeare's recusant relatives – Comparison of A.'s handwriting with Shakespeare's signatures   95

CHAPTER XI
Introduction to the genealogical charts   109

APPENDIX I
Five Genealogical charts, by Norman Long-Brown and Frances Keen   126

APPENDIX II
Transcription of the Annotations   127

CONTENTS

APPENDIX III
Examination of the Handwriting, by H. T. F. Rhodes — 151

APPENDIX IV
Prognosis on a Shakespeare Problem, by A. P. Rossiter (*Reprinted from* Durham University Journal, *March* 1941) — 164

APPENDIX V
A Model for Malvolio, by Beatrice Lilley — 186

APPENDIX VI
Alexander Aspinall — 195

APPENDIX VII
A Note on the Frontispiece — 199

APPENDIX VIII
Shropshire — 202

APPENDIX IX
Lancashire — 205

APPENDIX X
The Newport copy of Halle's Chronicle — 209

INDEX — 212

ILLUSTRATIONS

Frontispiece
THE GRAFTON PORTRAIT

Plate I
A TYPICAL PAGE
facing page 20

Plate II
SOME ANNOTATIONS
facing page 21

Plate III
SIR THOMAS HESKETH
facing page 36

Plate IV
THE EARL OF DERBY
facing page 37

Plate V
LORD STRANGE
facing page 84

Plate VI
WILLIAM FARINGTON
facing page 85

Plate VII
COMPARISON OF HANDWRITING
facing page 100

Plate VIII
COMPARISON OF HANDWRITING (*cont.*)
facing page 101

PREFACE

IT is over ten years since the start of investigations into the mystery of *who wrote in the margin*. The claim here advanced is that the writer was William Shakespeare. The reader's patience is invited, for he must suffer himself to be entangled in the network of Shakespearian connexions in order to appreciate our contention that the writer of the marginalia in the Newport copy of Halle's *Chronicle* was the young Shakespeare. Our exploration will endeavour to show the signposts in the progress of the fourteen-year-old boy, who, we believe, did *not* leave his native Stratford to hold horses' heads outside the Bankside playhouses, but was occupied in an environment and with associations more likely to encourage literary and historical inventiveness.

Those who have followed Alan Keen's researches since 1940 from the occasional bulletins that have appeared in the press, may recall how several years ago he declared that the apparent dissimilarity in form between the marginalia and Shakespeare's acknowledged signatures had convinced him that the notes could not, in fact, have been made by Shakespeare. Expert opinion which we now quote has since shown that conclusion to have been premature.

We include in the Appendices, by kind permission of the author, an analysis by A. P. Rossiter of what Shakespearian scholars might expect to find in marginal notes made by the young Shakespeare.

PREFACE

This appeared in the *Durham University Journal* soon after the news of the discovery of the notes first went abroad, in March 1941. It has been reprinted without alteration. It will be seen that in fact the notes differ in nature from the comments postulated by Mr Rossiter. The extent of the difference may suggest a measure of what these notes, if they are accepted as Shakespeare's, will contribute to the knowledge of Shakespeare's personality.

This book does not for a moment set itself up to be the final answer to the riddle of 'the hidden years'; but it does appear with the hope that it will stimulate reconsideration of the question.

In the course of the work many people came forward with help and encouragement. Our thanks and acknowledgment are due to: Lord Hesketh, descendant of the family which plays a great part in our narrative; Mr Noel Blakiston; Mr Stephen Potter; Mr John Bignell; Mr Augustus John, O.M., R.A.; Dr R. F. Rattray; Mr Ivor Brown; Miss Diana Neill; Mr J. M. Nosworthy of the University of Wales; Mr Jack Blakiston; Mr R. B. Halliday; Dr Francis Neilson, of New York; Mr R. Sharpe France, F.S.A., F.R.Hist.S.; Mr Selwyn Jepson; Dr A. W. Titherley; Mr David Hardman; Professor R. C. Bald; Mr Philip Ashcroft; Mr Ivor Kerrison Preston; Mr C. David Ley of the University of Madrid (whose book *Shakespeare para Espanoles*, 1951, summarises the present discoveries); Mr Geoffrey Brown, O.B.E.; Mr and Mrs S. W. Howard, of Croydon; Mr Rupert Jarvis, F.S.A.; Mr Christopher Callaghan; Dr J. H. Walter; Mr F. C. Willson; Mr F. C. Francis, British Museum;

PREFACE

and last, but by no means least, Mrs Peggy Hoare who has cheerfully endured countless revisions of the typescripts over the decade of work, and Mrs Jane Montgomery.

Of the two of us, it is Alan Keen that has played the principal detective's part in these last ten years of the story. It has therefore seemed convenient to present this report as his narrative: the 'I' of this book is Alan Keen. Since 1951 writing and investigation has in fact been equally shared. Argument has been hot, and collaboration happy.

November 1953

A.K.
R.J.L.

THE ANNOTATOR

I

I'll to my book;
For yet, ere supper-time must I perform
much business appertaining
                    (TEMPEST 3.1.94)

IN terram salicam mulieres ne succedant. . . . I had opened the old book at random; the Latin tag in the first act of Shakespeare's *Henry V*, already distinguished from the gothic text by its roman typeface, caught my eye, and held it. For the phrase was underlined in ink, now brown with age, and in the margin against it some Elizabethan had written, *note the exposition*.

Thumbing through centuries-old books is a routine matter for many people – certainly for an antiquarian bookseller running a professional eye over his purchase of a country library 'just in', as I was doing on 22 June 1940. Countless books from this particular library had on that day been opened and closed by my assistant and me, to be sorted and separated, until it fell to my lot to open the shabby folio, opening also (though I did not then know it) a detective story which has now lasted over ten years.

1940. An old book, however curious, could hardly seem to have much significance on that summer afternoon, when in the sky over Kent the vapour trails of the 'few' were annotating a new page in our proud history. But it was warm at the hall window of my Gate House in Clifford's Inn, and when the telephone bell called me to the comparative cool of my office I settled down to a closer examination of the thick folio volume.

It was a copy of the *Chronicle* of Edward Halle. If the title-page hadn't been missing I could have read the opening fanfare of the Tudor historian:

> 'The union of the two noble and illustrate famelies of Lancastre & Yorke, beyng long in continuall discension for the croune of this noble realme, with all the actes done in both the tymes of the Princes, both of the one linage & of the other, beginnyng at the tyme of kyng Henry the fowerth, the first aucthor of this devision, and so successively proceading to ye reigne of the high and prudent Prince Kyng Henry the eyght, the indubitate flower and very heire of both the saied linages.'

The book lacked a further leaf at the beginning, but the missing text had been supplied by an early nineteenth century owner who evidently prized this copy (imperfect as it was when it came into his possession) and wished to preserve it. In a meticulous, even clerkly hand, he had noted the edition and imperfections on the inside of the upper cover. An earlier owner had had the book cheaply rebound in boards covered with marbled paper and backed with calf, an operation which had shortened the margins of the copy, as the binder had trimmed the worn edges of the leaves. He had unfortunately, but inevitably, also 'cropped', or cut into, a number of the marginal notes by the unknown Elizabethan annotator. An eighteenth century library ticket, bearing the printed pressmark **EEd.** was pasted lower down in the inside of the upper cover, but no other evidence of ownership was to be found.

It seemed odd to me, a bookseller, that so unsatisfactory a copy of Halle should be preserved at a time when rare books in perfect state were as plentiful as blackberries, and I began to wonder why. Could it have been for the interest of the marginal notes, which I now observed were freely sprinkled over a great number of the earlier pages of the book? I began to decipher the handwriting, and to study the notes in relation to the text. They did not seem those of a casual commentator; rather as if designed to plot and summarise the 'lustye and flourishing stile' of the chronicler, to give point to the action and pageantry of the Wars of the Roses. Late afternoon found me still at work on the folio, surrounded by reference books; my four o'clock tea cold in its cup. When dinner-time approached I searched out a decrepit old portmanteau, placed the mysterious folio and the reference books in it, and made for Charing Cross.

Many were the quivers of excitement that old book, with its brittle crackling spine, gave me during the next hours and days, and many the critical friends against whose doubts I tried its mettle . . . but for the purposes of this tale, first things first: and the next stage was clearly to see if the marginal notes were as old as they pretended to be.

August 2nd found me with Dr Plenderleith in the British Museum Research Laboratory. This kindly Scot, pre-eminent in his vast field of scientific investigation, showed me how he had subjected the faded brown handwriting to infra-red and ultra-violet ray tests. With extreme delicacy he removed an infinitesimal speck of ink from one of the more strongly written of the notes, and showed me, through the microscope, a certain crystallisation of the ink. Then he handed me his certificate:

Research Laboratory,
British Museum,
London, W.C.1.

Mr Alan Keen.

I have examined the marginal annotations in Edward Halle 'Chronicle' 1550 (Pressmark EEd) and am of the opinion that those in ink are of considerable antiquity and were probably made all about the same time.

H. J. Plenderleith
2.8.40.

The notes were not a forgery: and they looked as if they had been written by a contemporary of Shakespeare.

Returning the folio to a friend, who had promised himself a leaf-by-leaf examination of the *whole* of the book, I plunged once again into the less exciting but necessary task of making a living. My business was growing in spite of air-raids and there was a good deal to be done with the State and University Libraries in the United States. My Gate House had a stoutly-built cellar below, and in the intervals between packing and reporting rare books, when the sirens wailed, my little staff and I went underground – often carrying our work with us, for the cellar had one useful electric bulb to relieve the gloom.

A telephone call from my friend brought good news. I hurried over to see him and not without pride he opened the folio in three places which he had marked with paper slips, to exhibit the undoubted proof of *original* ownership. In a hand completely different from that of the annotator, a certain *Rychard Newport* had written his name twice in the blank margins (many leaves after the annotated portion) of the book. On another leaf he had, bless him, put his initials with the date '6 *Apll. ao* 1565'. Here at last was our first major step towards that sober word 'provenance' – a word which may spell so much when it opens up a clue. The first part of my quest was to be the identification of the owner; who *was* Rychard Newport?

Inquiry into the Calendar of State Papers *Domestic*, gave us *two* men of that name, contemporaries, living in the sixteenth century. One Richard Newport was owner of Hunningham in Warwickshire from 1544 to his death on November 11th 1565. He could have owned this copy of Halle's *Chronicle*. This Richard Newport, we discovered also, through the marriage of his daughter and various other ties, was closely connected with the prominent Warwickshire family of Underhill, one of whom, his son-in-law, in 1567, when William Shakespeare was three years old, bought New Place, the 'great house' of Stratford-on-Avon. His son sold New Place to Shakespeare in 1597.

THE ANNOTATOR

This association looked intriguing. But the shadowy figure of the other Richard Newport was still at our elbow; there was no means of despatching him short of comparison of the *Chronicle* signatures with those of the two Newports, and this was impossible, for the State Papers were buried in the heart of the country for the duration of the war. So we had to shelve this nice problem until the more urgent one posed by Hitler had been dealt with. We could, however, get on with the investigation of the marginalia themselves.

II

What is thy name, young man?
(AS YOU LIKE IT, 1.2.233)

WHAT sort of man was he, this assiduous annotator of the margins of my Halle? A first inspection of his jottings revealed few signs of character; but perseverance was clearly necessary to find any gleams of light upon his personality that his notes might yield.

In the first place, he was a young man, writing in the latter half of the sixteenth century. Mr H. T. F. Rhodes, who contributes to this volume an expert 'examination' which appears as Appendix iii, opines that the writing has not yet attained its settled form, and points out that it consists of exactly that mixture of Gothic and Roman forms, predominantly Gothic, which was characteristic of the hand of Shakespeare and his contemporaries. It is basically the provincial 'secretary cursive' hand used by Shakespeare in his signatures, and by the scribe of a manuscript section of *Sir Thomas More*, said by some to be Shakespeare's.

Next, the annotator (we shall henceforth call him A.) was a very attentive student. He made laborious notes running to three thousand six hundred words, carefully extracting the pith and pattern of Halle's history, signposting details for easy reference, and only very rarely expressing his own views.

The book that he so intently perused was the

Fourth Issue of a history first published in 1548, and reissued the same year by Richard Grafton, scholar and printer, who made additions and was responsible for the subsequent issues. Edward Halle (or Hall), a Shropshire man educated at Eton and King's, Cambridge, was not simply intending to record events when he wrote *The Union of the Noble and Illustre Famelies of Lancastre and York*; he was going to produce one of the most ambitious works of propaganda of the century, making plain the frightful destruction that inevitably follows rebellion and civil dissension, and proving that the Union was successfully incarnated in the reigning monarch. Halle was a fervent Protestant, and his work was designed to help Henry VIII to scotch such subversive elements as should yet dare to raise their heads, and to confound anyone who questioned his authority, either spiritual or temporal. The author felt it his duty to free English history from the prejudices of monastic writing and the misrepresentations of foreign historians. He wished to set out the difficulties, tragedies and turmoils of the previous century as a warning and a lesson to his own age. Until the publication of Holinshed some thirty years later, his was the only English book in the field, and Holinshed drew largely upon it.

The *Chronicle* covered the period of history which was to be the age most often written about in the literature of the Elizabethans, notably in Shakespeare's Histories. Professor Dover Wilson says that Halle in a sense 'stretched the canvas and furnished the frame for the whole Shakespearian cycle,

THE ANNOTATOR

Richard II to *Richard III*', and it is now generally recognised that Shakespeare, besides his assiduous use of Holinshed, also used Halle as the direct source of various passages (e.g. *Richard II* 5.2). The whole evidence is set out in detail in Dr Gordon Zeeveld's *The Influence of Halle on Shakespeare's Historical Plays* (E.L.H., III, 1936).

Our student, A., seems to have been torn between sympathy with Halle's patriotic enthusiasm and fury at his anti-Catholicism, but he did not let his personal opinions intrude upon his thorough study: he made four hundred and six marginal notes, as well as sundry crosses and underlinings, and only some twenty-four of the notes can be considered in any way as comment. He never cites another authority: as he shows himself to be studious, intelligent, and a persistent annotator, one surmises that this was his first reading in the subject.

His method is best displayed by example. He was evidently struck by Halle's account of Richard II's abdication speech to the assembly at the Tower, a passage which runs to 52 lines (H.iv.f.ix).[1] The first four describe Richard's appearance in robes of state: the next thirty report his speech: then his presentation of the crown and sceptre to Lancaster Bolingbroke, his request for mercy, his pledge of his personal fortune 'to the some of three hundred thousand pounde in coyne, besyde plate and iuels'; and the passage winds up, 'shortly after his resignacion he was conueighed to the Castell of Ledes

---

[1] We shall abbreviate references to the text of Halle in this manner, 'H.iv.f.ix' means Folio ix of *The Unquiet Time of King Henry IV*

in Kent, and from thence to Poumffret where he departed out of this miserable life.'

At the head of the paragraph A. noted '*A solempne resignation of the crowne by King Richard*'. (His use of 'resignation' suggests that he had read to the end before returning to make the note.) Next, where Richard pleads that his failure in 'royal office and bounden duty' was caused by 'sinister counsaill of peruerse & flattering persones . . . the frailtie of young wauering and wanton youth, and with delectacion of worldly and voluptuous appetite', A. put in the margin, '*Nota for flaterye & wanton & voluptuose pleasure*' – here he evidently wished to remember a pointer to the psychology and character of the King, rather than any particular incident.

His next note, towards the end of the speech, is of a contrasting character, simply extracting a detail, '*A gret some of money delivered* 300000 *li*.' He began to make this note, as was his practice, at the head of the long sentence containing the point; but then presumably feeling that this was a detail and not a general summary, he moved down eight lines and jotted it exactly opposite its appearance in the text.

Another speech that evidently caught A.'s attention is that of the Constable of France to his Captains before Agincourt (H.v.f.xvi). About halfway through it, A. abstracted the general sense and tone of the speech: '*An oration of ther captayne against the englisshe armye . . . moche coragiose.*' Earlier, the arrogance of the Constable 'we cannot but be victours', had driven A.'s patriotic pen to note petulantly, '*pryde hadde a fall*'. The Constable's estimation of the English character evidently struck him, for he next picked out one aspect of the speech, '*The frenche man notethe the nature of the englisshe man*'. Finally, following his general summary he made concise reminders of the Constable's exhortatory argument: '*first affirminge the englisshe armye weake . . . seconde the defacinge of the bloude . . . Thrydde the riches of the englisshe camp.*'

These are not the kind of illuminating comments and comparisons that a subsequent reader is glad to find in a margin; nor are they of the infuriating 'what bosh!' type; they are more methodical than that. They are not all simple cross-headings, pointers left to the information available in the book. They are not even the casual nota-benes of a man intent on his own erudition – the selection of that striking detail, the exact total of Richard's fortune, would be of no value to him: nor, on the other hand, does the interest in Richard's character suggest a compiler of statistics.

Evidently A. intended to return to the book – '*Nota for flaterye*' could hardly suggest anything else – and already he seems to have had some purpose in view, an approximate idea of what he wanted to get from the book. These notes appear to be the signposts left by a thoughtful and methodical reader, who was planning to use a selection of the material for some purpose of his own.

A. was intent to learn rather than to criticise, thus leaving us little trace of his own personality:

but every now and then he did let his pen run just a few words away with him. For instance, he was a real jingo of a patriot, and hated the French. '*vi M* (six thousand) *frenchmen assaulted iii C* (three hundred) *englisshe men & gatte no honour*' – so much for them! '*Note the kowardyce of the frenche men*'; '*A cowardlye acte of cvi horsemen of fraunce*'; '*weake aunswer of the dolphin*' – one senses A.'s terse satisfaction. (Another gloss, '*lamentable verses made by the parisians*' seems to strike the same note in a curiously modern key – but I'm afraid we must not read it so!)

Yet more emphatically, A. had a strong Roman Catholic, even clerical, bias. Halle often let himself go with eloquence and enthusiasm on the baseness, dishonesty, avarice, power, and general undesirability of priests, cardinals, and Popes, and A. did not let these passages pass unnoticed. Halle wrote: 'The most ambicious desire and avaricious appetite of certayne persones callyng themselves spiritual fathers, but indeede carnall covetous and gredy glottons aspiring for honor and not for vertue to the proud see of Rome', and A. would not stand for that: '*The Author (if he dyd write it) wrote it in the afternoone.*' When Halle told of the first rebellion against Henry IV, expressing himself at length and bitterly against monastical persons better fed than taught, and imagining their vituperations against any prince who might justly reclaim some part of their possessions, A. commented: '*here he begynneth to rayle.*' '*Allways lying,*' he said of another tirade of Halle's against 'proud priors'.

He shewed a sympathy for clergy in general: of the Bishop of Carlisle's speech in defence of

THE ANNOTATOR

Richard II, '*The bisshop of Carleile spake to late but yet very stoutlye*'; but mostly such sympathy was reserved for clergy who opposed the temporal powers, and when Halle described Henry V's Archbishop of Canterbury as a 'man muche regardyng Godes law, but more louying his own lucre', A. only put a double cross; perhaps one of approval. A. betrayed his own allegiance most clearly in, '*Note that when he speakethe of the Pope he sheweth himself of the englisshe schisme a favorer*' (when Halle writes of 'the Romishe bishop'). Once, he even let his Catholic loyalty stand before his patriotism: '*a stowt bisshop of fraunce so in defiaunce of a prince to speke.*'

An interesting point about these 'religious' comments is that most of them have been either written over previous erasions (possibly still stronger in tone) or half-heartedly obscured by A.'s own pen. Did he repent of them, or was it simply natural caution in an age when recusants went to the stake? If so, why write them at all, and why then erase them so ineffectively? Of this, Moray McLaren has convincingly written,

> The answer seems to me to be quite clear. The annotator was a type which has been quite common in these Islands ever since the Reformation. I refer not to the completely lapsed Catholic, but to the man who, brought up in a fervently Catholic atmosphere, gradually drifts away from his duties and practices, either through laziness or semi-scepticism. Nevertheless the Catholic philosophy has so entered into his mentality that if he is faced with a Protestant or Atheistical argument he will be the first to leap into the *verbal* defence of the faith.

One of the few annotations that present any obscurity seems to fall into the group of these religious comments. Halle recounts that before Agincourt an Englishman, 'a foolishe souldier, stole a pixe out of a church and unreverently did eate holy hostes within the same conteigned. For whiche cause he was apprehended and the Kynge would not once remove till the vessel was restored and the offender strangled.' (An incident which Holinshed also mentions, probably lifting it from Halle, and which Shakespeare embodies in the misfortunes of poor Bardolph:

Fortune is Bardolph's foe, and frowns on him:
For he hath stolen a pax and hanged must a' be.)

Against this incident, A. has written: '*A cryme committyd & if this boke had had one author it wold not have bene noted/nam oportet mendacem esse memorem.*' ('For it behoves a liar to be mindful.') A.'s suggestion is presumably that Halle, being so virulently and deceitfully anti-Catholic, would not have admitted to his record this display on Henry V's part of respect to the Faith; but that a subsequent editor included it.

The next note I made on A'.s personality concerned his taste for catch-phrases and doggerel. His first entry of all, a summary of Halle's whole mighty argument, he has derived from the chronicler's 'as by discorde great thynges decaie and fall to ruyne, so the same by concorde be revived and erected', and has made it,

> *by concorde smalle*
> *thinges doithe growe*
> *by discorde gret thinges*
> *dothe awaye flowe*

'Lamentable verses' indeed!

He jots down another jingle in two forms: *'he that wyll fraunce wynne with scotland he must begynne'*, and *'he that wille scotland wynne let him with france first begynne'*. Shakespeare, incidentally, uses this adage in the form,

> If that you will France win
> Then with Scotland first begin.
> (HENRY V, 1.2.167)

His interest in adages also appears in a comment against Halle's 'I Henry borne at Monmoth shall small tyme reigne & muche get, & Henry borne at Wyndsore shall long reigne and all lese . . .' (H.v.f. xlvi) – of which Shakespeare makes

> And now I fear that fatal prophecy
> Which in the time of Henry named the fifth
> Was in the mouth of every sucking babe:
> That Henry born at Monmouth should win all
> And Henry born at Windsor lose all.
> (I HENRY VI, 3.1)

A. noticed it with, *'A notable sayeinge of two Kinge henrys'*.

When Halle tells how the Earl of Armagnac raised his siege of Harfleur, 'and returned with small ioy to Parus, as he that had no hope', A. comments tersely: *'The earle of arminacke retorned to parice with a flea in his eare.'* 'Pryde hadde a fall' we have seen. Of the French nobles' professed admiration of Henry after his victory, A. remarks '*A padde in the straw, peradventure.*'

A. took some interest in military matters and equipment. He noticed a long catalogue in the text, of 'helme, visere, bavier, plackardes, port, burley' and so on, with the signpost, '*the names of sondry pieces of armour*'. Elsewhere, '*the souldiers did mete clothe with ther bowes*'.

He put an interesting comment against the passage in which Halle describes (H.v.f.xvii) how before Agincourt the King 'caused stakes bound with yron sharpe at both endes of the length of V or VI fote, to be pitched before the Archers and of euery side the foote men like an hedge, to the extent that if the varde horses ranne rashely upon them, they might shortely be gored and destroied.'

Against this A. wrote rather ambiguously: '*The inventynge of stakes which now I thinke be morres pykes.*' Morris, or Moorish, pikes were sixteenth century weapons of the type that Halle describes: Shakespeare was familiar with them, making Dromio of Syracuse speak of one who 'sets up his rest to do more exploits with his mace than a morris-pike' (*C. of E.*, 4.3.25). Such weapons, however, were certainly not known by this name at the time of Agincourt. What A. has done in this case is to note a modern equivalent: as nowadays a military-minded reader might write against an account of the use of boiling oil in a medieval siege, 'Cf. present use of Crocodile' (which is a flame-throwing tank).

However, A. was by no means blind to the grim side of war. '*A pitiuse case*', he sorrowfully exclaims, '*dogges rattes cattes and myse eaten*'! (during the siege of Rouen). '*Prisoners pitifully slayne*'; and on the other hand, of Henry V at Caen restraining his soldiers from looting the citizens' abandoned treasure, he noted, '*A noble and notable acte of pytie.*'

That is all we could make out about A. from his notes; others more clairvoyant, better psychologists, or simply more learned in Elizabethan matters, may be able to discover more of the personality of this eager young scribbler we have called A. Who, oh who, was he?

It might be suggested that he was a fan of the Elizabethan playhouse, who was reading over Halle to check up on Shakespeare's historical accuracy, after he had seen some of that author's History plays. But this will not do, for he annotates a lot of Halle that Shakespeare does not use: for instance, the account of the fortunes of Scotland in the middle of Henry IV's reign (H.iv.f.xxvi-xxviii); here A. notes such striking incidents as '*Walter governer of Scotland hongersterved his nephew David the prince & kylled a woman that gave him mylke of hir brestes with a rede*'.

The similarity of A.'s historical interest and attitude to Shakespeare's is, to say the least of it, intriguing. Of course, as Shakespeare derived much of his historical knowledge, directly or via Holinshed from Halle, a general similarity of theme would not be surprising, but there is more to it than that.

A., like Shakespeare, and Halle, was convinced that 'civil dissention' was something to be feared and avoided. '*Note for the love of foren princes*', he

THE ANNOTATOR

writes, *'that it defendythe from civile sedition'* – and we know what a nationalist he was! *'Divisyon had almost decayed fraunce with utter ruyne'*; *'marke the yssew of cyvyle dissention'*; and of the pre-eminent example, *'Dyvisyon ones entred never ended tyll the heares males of bothe the houses yorke & lancastre were destroyed'*.

 England hath long been mad, and scarr'd herself;
 The brother blindly shed his brother's blood,
 The father rashly slaughter'd his own son,
 The son compell'd been butcher to the sire:
 All this divided York and Lancaster
 Divided in their dire division . . .

The faint requiem of a muted trumpet seems to echo in my ears. . . .

 A., like Shakespeare, paid particular attention to the character of monarchs, their rights and their careers. *'Nota for flaterye'* we have mentioned. Also of Richard II he notes, *'lacke of assured and friendly com . . .'* (the note is cropped). This detail, reflecting upon the King, is the only point A. selects to remember from a passage (H.iv.f.iv) dealing with the Duke of York's withdrawal to a resting place. *'Kynge Richard fought manfullye befor deathe as some saye'*; and, *'Two Kinges for lacke of sober sadnes brogt to calamitye. Ric 2 Edward 2'*, are other notes of the same tendency.

 At King Henry IV's death he made a note typical of his concise summarising: *'Kinge henrye semithe to confesse that he had the crowne wrongefullye & died anno domini 1413. he raigned xiii yeares & v monethes. buryed at canterburye.'* Shakespeare, too, saw significance in this misgiving of the dying king. He made Henry IV, on his death-bed, tell his eldest son:

THE ANNOTATOR

> God knows, my son,
> By what by-paths and indirect, crook'd ways
> I met this crown . . . It seem'd in me
> But as an honour snatch'd with boisterous hand. . .

A. took note of the transformation in Prince Henry's character that Shakespeare hinged so much upon: '*honours brought to the Kynge good maners*'; and of the full character attained by Henry V at the end of his life, was as admiring as one imagines Shakespeare would have been: '*with his vertues & good parties manifold and wonderfull rare . . . his activitye . . . his temperance . . . his corage . . . his pollicye . . . his bountifulnes . . .*'

Extracting the pith of Halle's conception of the majestical influence of kings, A. noted, '*The frenchemens power was weak bycause their Kynges wit was not stronge*'; and in another place, using a phrase of his own not taken from Halle, even more tersely and pregnantly summed up his own faith in the monarchical principle: '*Such prince suche people.*'

III

He echoes me . . .
(OTHELLO, 3.3.106)

THERE was no resisting the temptation to see how much further the Shakespearian parallel could be carried. Indeed, I could not help asking myself, are these Shakespeare's notes? Could this have been Shakespeare's work-book?

Certainly we do not find, in these marginal scribbles, any sign of the flashing imagination, the sinewy style, 'the evident pulse of a powerful mind', that we look for in every sentence that Shakespeare wrote. But as we have seen, the annotator was here out to learn, not to entertain: and if these notes were made by Shakespeare, they would have come from his pen several years earlier than any of his writing that survives.

Who can surmise what kind of a man Shakespeare was at seventeen? Looking into the minds and development of any of the Elizabethans, we at once find ourselves groping about a bewildering maze of sliding clues and assertive improbabilities. In Shakespeare's particular case, as far as we know he wrote nothing before he was twenty-five; and at that inauspicious age started out on ten years' development whose staggering pace and extent all the world can judge by comparing *The Comedy of Errors* with *As You Like It*. Such development fits into no known pattern: there is no progressive

Kyng Henry the v. Fo. xxi.

issue, whiche was an happy chaunce for Robynet of Bournoule and his compaignions as you haue hearde before, for his deathe was their life, and his life would haue been their death.

¶ The .iiii. yere.

After this notable victory obteined by the Englishmen & ḡ kyng Henry was departed into England, & the Frēche kyng had made newe officers in hope to releue & set vp againe the old estate of his realme & countrey, Thomas duke of Excester capitain of Harflew accōpanied with thre M. Englishmen made a great road into Normandy, almoste to thee city of Roan: In whiche iorney he gat great habundaunce bothe of riches and prisoners. But in his returne theele of Irminacke newly made Constable of Fraunce, entendyng in his first iorney to wynne his spurres, and in his compaignie aboue. v. M. horssemen, encountred with hym. The skirmishe was sore and the fight fierse, but because the Englishemen wer not able to resyfte the force of the Frenche Horssemen, the Duke to saue his men was compelled to retire, as polleticquely as he could deuise: But for all that he could do he lost almost .ccc. of his foremen. The Frenchmen not content with this good lucke folowed theim almoste too thee Barriers of Harflew. When the Englishemen within the toune espied the chase, ther issued oute in good ordre and met with their enimies, and not onely slew and toke a greate numbre of them, but also chased theym aboue eyghte miles toward the citee of Roan.

Aboute this ceason Sigismond Emperour of Almayne whiche had maried Barbara doughter to theele of Xilie cosyn germayn remoued to kyng Henry (as by the pedegree set out in the end of this boke you shall plainly perceiue) a man of greate vertue and fidelitie, whiche had not only long labored to set an vnitie and concord in Christes Churche and christian religion, but also he sent diuers Ambassadors aswel to ḡ Frēch kyng as to the kyng of Englande, because he was farre distaunt from their countreies and regions to encrease perfight peace and reasonable vnitie. Wherfore, seyng that his Ambassade broughte nothyng to conclusion he in person came frō the farthest part of Hungary into Fraunce and after into England, intendyng to knit together all christian prynces in one line and amitee, and so beyng frendes together, to make warre and reuenge their quarrelles against the Turk the persecutor of Christes faithe and enemie to all christendome. With this noble Ēmperor came the Archebushoppe of Repnes and diuerse other noble men, as Ambassadors frō the Frenche kyng into Englande. The kyng of Englande for old amitee betwene the hous of Englande and Beame, withall hys nobilitie hym receiued on Blackheth the .bii. date of Maie, and brought him through London to Westminster with greate triumphe, where Iustes, tournayes and other materiall feates were to hym with all joye
D.iii. and

PLATE II

appareed, for he had onely two. M. horsemen and. ruj. M. Archers, but men and of all sortes. The Englishemen were afflicted in this iourney with an hundred discomodities, for their vitaile was in maner al spent, and newe they could gette none, for their enemies had destroyed all the corne before their compyng: Best they could take none, for theyr enemies wer euer at hande, Daily it reined and nightly itfresed, of fuell was ska cenes and of flures was plenty, money they had ynough but comforte thei had none. And yet in this greate necessitee the pore folkes wer not spopled nor any thyng wythout paiment was of the extorted, nor great offence was doen except one, whiche was that a foolishe souldier stale a pire out of a churche and vnreuerently did eate the holy hostes with: in thesame conteigned. For whiche cause he was apprehended, and the kyng would not once remoue till the vessel was restored & the offender stranngled. The people of the countrees there aboute hearyng of hys straight iustice & godly mynd, ministered to hym bothe vitailes & other necessaries, although by open proclamacio they wer therof prohibited.

1. A section of H.v. f.xva. The note, 'A cryme committyd and if this boke had had one author it wold not have bene noted/nam oportet mendacem esse memorem', is referred to in Ch. II. The 'doodle' in the opposite margin, possibly referring to the 'foolishe souldier', is referred to in Appendix X.

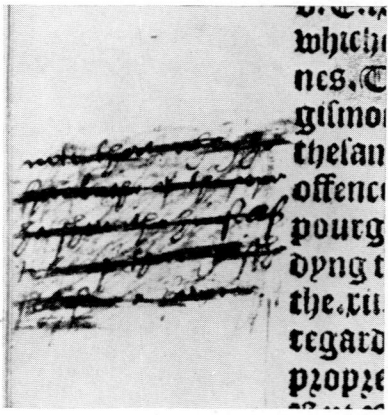 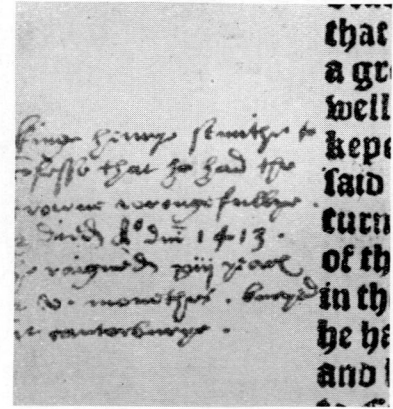

2. One of the overscored notes referred to in Ch. II. From H.v. f.iiia, 'note that when he speakethe of the pope he shewithe himself to be of the englisshe schisme a favorer.'

3. From H.iv. f.xxxiii, shewing use of roman and arabic numerals. 'Kinge henrye semithe to confesse that he had the crowne wrongefullye and died Ao dni 1413. he raigned xiii yeares and v monethes. buryed at canterburye.'

SOME ANNOTATIONS

series we can extend backwards, to chart the range of his mind in earlier years.

There is no doubt that A.'s selection of material and his eye for character were strikingly like Shakespeare's: often, too, his singling out of Halle's words. We have already quoted examples where A.'s pick of Halle's words is repeated by Shakespeare: *'he that wyll fraunce wynne . . .'*, and the underlining, with *'note the exposition'*, of 'In terram salicam mulieres ne succedant'.

There are a good many such instances, where a detail or expression is selected from Halle by A. and also used, verbatim or in the same general sense, by Shakespeare. The text of the plays alone, however, gives good grounds for thinking that Shakespeare had Halle's *Chronicle* in his memory when he wrote the History plays, and sometimes even had it beside him. Dr Zeeveld writes:

> The evidence so far presented indicates that Shakespeare utilized Hall as well as Holinshed in the English historical plays; but there is also evidence to show that Shakespeare gave dramatic expression to the very qualities in Hall's history which later historians rejected or ignored: the elevation of style by means of oration and rhetorical figure, liveliness of narrative detail, development of character and motive, and the denomination of theme in the establishment of continuity in fifteenth century history.

Verbal echoes of Halle, cropping up here and there about the plays, suggest that Shakespeare had in fact read the *Chronicle* carefully enough for fragments of it to lodge in his memory. For instance,

Boyet in *Love's Labour's Lost*, 4.1, reads out to the Princess an intercepted letter from the fantastic Armado: 'The magnanimous and most *illustrate* King Cophetua set eye upon the pernicious and *indubitate* beggar Zenelophon. . . .' 'I am much deceived but I remember this style', remarks Boyet, and so may we, casting our minds back to Halle's opening flourish, 'The Union of the two noble and *illustr(at)e* famelies of Lancastre and Yorke . . . proceading to the reigne of the High and prudent Prince King Henry the Eighth, the *indubitate* and very heire of the said linages.'

'*Cum privilegio ad imprimendum solum*' is a phrase that Shakespeare might have lifted from a good many books for Biondello's 'Take you assurance of her "cum privilegio ad imprimendum solum" to the church; take the priest, clerk, and some sufficient honest witnesses' (*Taming of the Shrew*, 4.4). It does, however, often occur in slight variants. Here Grafton has it pat:

IMPRYNTED AT LONDON BY
Rychard Grafton, Prynter to the Kynges Maiestye
1550
Cum priuilegio ad imprimendum solum.

Another minute but telling supporter of the theory that Shakespeare was sometimes writing with Halle open beside him comes from a misprint on H.v.f.iv*b*, where Halle has '. . . betwene the riuers of Elue and Sala'. Holinshed gets the river right, 'Elbe'; but Shakespeare apparently follows Halle in his error, and the First Folio text (the 'true' text for *Henry V*) has 'Betweene the Flouds of Sala and of Elue'. Professor Dover Wilson, in his preface to the play, concedes this as a pointer to the direct use of Halle.

So the selection of one of Halle's words or details by A. and its similar use by Shakespeare, does not by itself tell us very much. Far more striking would clearly be any example of the use by A. of a word *not* occurring in Halle that *is* used by Shakespeare in the equivalent passage.

We saw in the last chapter what careful attention A. gave to the exhortatory speech of the Constable of France before Agincourt (H.v.f.xvi); when he made this series of notes, A. seems to have been inclined to use his own words rather than borrow Halle's. Now, these two pages of my annotated *Chronicle* became my favourite reading when one of my persistently sceptical and erudite acquaintances had dashed a high-flying hope I had ventured to utter – for every one of these words was used by Shakespeare, most of them in the History plays, and several of them in the exactly equivalent passages.

After Halle has recounted the general situation and time of the battle (and A. has noted them accordingly), he writes: 'It was a glorious syght to behold them, and surely they wer estemed to be in numbre sixe times as many or more then was the whole compaigny of the Englishmen wyth wagoners, pages, and all.' A. glosses, in words nowhere used by Halle, *'gret oddes betwene the englisshe armye & the frenche'*. 'Odds' is often used by Shakespeare, and a notable example occurs in the conversation among the English generals before Agincourt (*Henry V*, 4.3):

EXETER: There's five to one: besides they are all fresh.[1]

SALISBURY: God's arm strike with us! 'tis a fearful odds.

A.'s next mark comes against the Constable's boast, 'For wee cannot but be victours and triumphant conquerors, for who saw ever so florisshyng an armie. . . .' Caustically wrote A., *'pryde hadde a fall'* – a phrase that is used by Shakespeare in *Richard II*, 5.5.88:

> Since pride must have a fall.

Next in the margin, A. signposted a feature of the speech that caught his fancy: '*The frenche man notethe the nature of the englisshe man*' – the 'nature' in this case being analysed by the Constable as: 'For you must understand, that kepe an Englishman one moneth from hys warme bed, fat befe and stale drynke, and let him that season tast cold and suffre hunger, you then shall se his courage abated, hys bodye waxe leane and bare, and euer desirous to returne into hys own countrey.'

Shakespeare put into the mouths of two of his Frenchmen before Agincourt just this absurdly larder-minded view of our countrymen (*Henry V*, 3.7):

ORLEANS: Ay, but these English are shrewdly out of beef.

CONSTABLE: Then shall we find tomorrow they have only stomachs to eat and none to fight.

---

[1] Where Halle says 'six', and Holinshed agrees, Shakespeare says 'five'. Could this have arisen from the fact that in Halle's rather cramped and blotchy black-letter, 'ſixe' would be easily misread as 'fiue' by the eye of a scanning reader intent mainly upon the marginal notes?

There is another allusion to this same French superstition in *I Henry VI*, 1.2:

> CHARLES: . . . the famish'd English like pale ghosts,
> Faintly besiege us one hour in a month.
> ALENCON: They want their porridge and their fat bull beves.

Next comes A.'s note of the Constable, *'moche coragiose'*: and then follow his three side-headings to the Constable's argument for hating and resisting the invaders: *'first affirminge the englisshe armye weake . . . seconde the defacinge of the bloude . . . Thrydde the riches of the englisshe campe.'*

'Affirm' is a good Shakespearian word, and we do not need to go far for an example:

> Yet their own authors faithfully affirm
> That the land Salique is in Germany
> (HENRY V, 1.2.43)

The second head is cryptic and intriguing. The Constable describes the English King's supposed plan for his conquest of France: 'then he and hys entende to occupy this countrey inhabite this lande, destroy our wiues and children, extinguishe our blud and put our names in the blacke boke of obliuion.'

In *Henry V*, the tenor of this speech as related by Halle runs through the conference in the French court in 2.4, being given to several speakers. To encourage his captains, the Constable (in Halle) describes to them the poor plight of the English owing to their beef-shortage, and says, 'therefore nowe, it is no mastery to vanquishe and ouerthrowe

THE ANNOTATOR

them, beyng bothe wery and weke . . . But ymagyn that they were lusty, strong and couragious, and then ponder wisely the cause of theyr comyng hither . . . Wherfore remember well, in what quarrel can you better fight . . .' Shakespeare makes the Dauphin say:

> In cases of defence 'tis best to weigh
> The enemy more mighty than he seems . . .

and the King goes on to recount, as does the Constable in Halle, the causes of the French anger, coming eventually to an effective use of 'deface', when he reminds them of the Black Prince, whose father:

> . . . smiled to see him
> Mangle the work of nature, and deface
> The patterns that by God and by French fathers
> Had twenty years been made.

Shakespeare has transmuted the prose argument into poetry; and he has brought in a word that does not appear in Halle's text, but *is* used in exactly Shakespeare's sense, by the annotator A., in his strikingly pregnant and strangely poetical phrase, *'the defacinge of the bloude'*.

Another example of the use by A. and Shakespeare of a word not Halle's, is:

> Halle: 'The Duke . . . sailed into England and landed at Rauenspurre' (H.iv.f.vi*a*).
> A.: *'the duke arryved in england at ravenspurre.'*
> Shakespeare: 'The banish'd Bolingbroke . . . is safe arriv'd at Ravenspurgh.'

'Banished' is a word used several times by A. In the account of the duel between Bolingbroke and

Mowbray, suddenly stopped by Richard II and concluding with sentences of exile all round, Halle only once uses the word 'banish'. Opposite this, A. notes, '*Henry duke of Herford banisshed for x years*'; and farther down, '*Thomas duke of norfolk banisshid for ever*'. One recalls how in *Richard II*, 1.3, the word chimes through the scene like a gloomy bell, from

> Therefore we banish you our territories:
> You, cousin Hereford, upon pain of life,
> Till twice five summers have enriched our fields,
> Shall not regreet our fair dominions,
> But tread the stranger paths of banishment,

and later,

> Lay on our royal sword your banished hands,
> Swear by the duty that you owe to God
> (Our part therein we banish with yourselves) . . .

to the last line,

> Though banished, yet a trueborn Englishman.

Again, in *II Henry IV*, the newly-crowned Henry V dismisses Falstaff and his hangers-on with,

> Till then I banish thee, on pain of death . . .
> Not to come near our person by ten mile.

In the margin of the *Chronicle*, A. (like Shakespeare using the singular 'mile' for 'miles'), made the relevant note (H.v.f.i.) '*All flatterers and olde companions banisshed x myle from the courte.*'

A.'s next marginal note also finds an echo. As Halle went on to say that in place of such 'old plaie felowes and procurers of al mischiefes and riot', Henry V appointed 'men of gravitee, persones of

THE ANNOTATOR

activitee, and counsayllers of grate witte and policie', A. summed it up with *'sage counsellers chosen'*. Now, Shakespeare's Henry IV, unhappily prophesying about this moment in his son's monarchy, said on his death-bed,

> Harry the fifth is crown'd: up, vanity!
> Down, royal state! all you sage counsellors, hence!

Another example of A. making note of some semi-proverbial tradition about a country or its people that was also adopted by Shakespeare (perhaps such proverbial attributes were truer in his day than they ever are now!) occurs on H.v.f. viii, where A. noted *'Scotland a contray barren of pleasure & goodness'*. In *The Comedy of Errors*, Antipholus of Syracuse asks his attendant in what part of Nell's body he will locate Scotland:

> DROMIO S.: I found it by the barrenness: hard, in the palm of the hand (C. OF E., 3.2.122).

The number of words that A. uses off his own bat, not borrowing from Halle, is limited; apart from the foregoing striking examples, it is noteworthy that almost all these words from A.'s own vocabulary are Shakespearian ones, used in a Shakespearian sense: *'complices'*; *'discomfytyd'*; *'gird against'*; *'a fetche'* meaning a stratagem; *'a brute of fame'*, where Halle has 'blased abrode and noysed'. (Shakespeare, 'I find thou art no less than fame hath bruited', *I Henry VI*, 2.3.68.) *'Sleveles'*; *'stomack'*. A. has *'dyd stomack the matter'*, where Halle says 'was sore moued with this chaunce'. (Shakespeare, "Tis not a time for private stomach-

28

ing', *A. and C.*, 2.2.9.) 'Reduce' in the sense of bringing back: A. summarised a long passage with the words, '*Scottland was therby reducyed from barbarose savagenes*', and Shakespeare has, 'Which to reduce into our former favour' (*Henry V*, 5.2.63).

'Slight' is in one place used in the same sense, and approximately the same situation, by A. and Shakespeare, not by Halle. In *Henry V*, 2.4, Exeter says he brings to the Dauphin,

Scorn and defiance: slight regard, contempt

and A. notes of the treatment Exeter receives, '*A sleight aunswer to the embassadours*'.

A.'s one piece of adventurous grammar, the elliptical '*Suche prince suche people*', for Halle's 'As kynges go, the subiectes folowe' (H.v.f.ii) cannot be exactly matched in Shakespeare (as far as I can find).

Alas, our frailty is the cause, not we:
For such as we are made of, such we be
(T.N., 2.2.33)

comes fairly near it.

Little wonder that perusal of the annotations made me feel that A. must somehow have had something to do with William Shakespeare. Might not this very book have been pored over by the playwright, and annotated by him in his youth, at the time when he was first thinking about writing the History plays? It was an idea that I could hardly dare to contemplate: for more than three centuries, a few signatures are all that has been found of Shakespeare's handwriting. This annotator's commentary would add up to pages of continuous script. Perhaps in the history of literature it is very unimportant to know what Shakespeare's early handwriting was like; but I found the idea intoxicating.

But how could this copy of the *Chronicle* have come into Shakespeare's hands? How could he have found his way into the New Place library as a youth? For it was there presumably that the Stratford boy would have been most likely to come across this copy of the *Chronicle,* in the house of its first owner's son-in-law. If not there, where *was* the book when A. made his notes? Or where was Shakespeare, if and when he made them?

There were no clues about the book's life apart from Newport's signatures and the library label. I determined to start from these and follow every scent that might blow my way.

IV

Any thing that is fitting to be known, discover.
(WINTER'S TALE, 4.4.740)

THE quest of Richard Newport had to be shelved until the war was over. At last the jubilant summer of 1945 arrived, and the State documents returned to their official residence in London. As soon as I could, I looked out the signatures of the two Newports. With sickening, though as I soon realised, unreasonable, disappointment, I found that the signatures in the *Chronicle* were not those of Richard Newport of Hunningham, the relative of the Underhills. The 'other' Newport presented himself. He was Sir Richard Newport, Lord of Ercall and Sheriff of Shropshire, who died in 1570. He was the early, probably the first, owner of our *Chronicle*. I sadly gave up my highest Shakespearian hopes, and concentrated on the new trail.

To my relief, facts about this remote Sir Richard Newport of High Ercall at first came easily to hand. He married Margaret, daughter and sole heir of Sir Thomas Bromley, Lord Chief Justice of England, and thus became owner of the great house at Eyton-on-Severn. Magdalen his daughter married Richard Herbert of Montgomery. She became a patroness of literature and friend of John Donne, and her two sons must have delighted her heart. Edward (later Lord Herbert of Cherbury), who received his education from a tutor in his grandfather's house at Eyton, lived to win honours by his wit and pen. George her second son, was destined to holy orders and a poet's laurels. The annotated *Chronicle*, had, it appeared, been within an ownership and succession of *readers*.

In my pursuit of the line of Newport, I was favoured by the appearance, late one afternoon, of Dick Halliday of Leicester who dropped in at the Gate House from the nearby Hodgson's Book Auction Rooms. Dick, who, with his brother Kenneth, succeeded to the fine business of Bernard Halliday on his father's death, specialises in county histories and genealogies. Over a cup of tea we gossiped, as is our habit, on the undying topic of new 'finds'. He had, I soon learned, attended the Lilford Sale at Sotheby's a couple of weeks before, and picked up an original manuscript *visitation* of Shropshire. Most certainly the Newports of High Ercall would occur, agreed Dick, and as he left for his train to Leicester, promised to post the manuscript to me on approval.

Two days later the parcel arrived, with slips of paper between the leaves of the volume where he had marked the Newport pedigrees and descents. That evening I examined the manuscript at leisure. It was inscribed:

The visitacon of Shropshire taken and made by Richard Lee / als Richmonde Heralde and Marshall to Robert / Cooke als Clarencieux Kinge of Armes taken in / the yeare of our lord god Ao. 1564 (& 1584) / Augmented by many notes and gatherings of Lewis Dwnn / and others by me Jacob Chaloner of London gent / untill this present yeare of our Lord god / Ao. 1620.

THE ANNOTATOR

In its smooth seventeenth-century calf binding, opening to the coloured blazons of bygone Shropshire families, with their 'trees' on each page, it was an attractive book, and made by an interesting herald. This Jacob Chaloner, who was apprenticed to his stepfather Randle Holme (Deputy to the College of Arms for Cheshire, Shropshire and North Wales, the Mayor of Chester, 1633-4) in 1607, was the eldest son of Thomas Chaloner of Chester, Ulster King of Arms, painter, poet, antiquary, and actor – he was a member of Lord Derby's company of players.

The Newport-Bromley-Herbert line appeared clearly enough in the pedigrees. The Newport tree joined that of the Leveson family, and at the juncture I noticed an entry of marriage: 'Sr. Richard Levesonne of Lilleshall Kt – Mary Da. to Sr. Edward Fitton of Cheshire Kt.'

This Mary proved to be the great-aunt of none other than Mary Fitton, the 'Dark Lady' of the Sonnets. Pondering further on the period of the 'Dark Lady's' life (1578-1647) during which I presume our annotator was at work, I recalled that Professor Hotson, in one of his books of hawk-eyed detective work on the background of Shakespeare, notices one member of the Leveson family resident in London – William Leveson, companion with John Heminges as Shakespeare's trustee and partner in the Globe Theatre.

Investigating the Fitton tree further, I found close connexion by marriage with the families of Houghton and Hesketh. Houghton and Hesketh! This conjunction of names rang another bell in my memory, with echoes we shall hear later.

It suffices to note for the moment that the families of Corbet, Newport, Bromley, Leveson, Vernon, Fitton, Arden, Holcroft, and Hesketh, were interrelated in a pattern which spread out from Shropshire to Lancashire and all over the Midlands. Richard Newport's possessions might have found their way into the homes of any of the families in this clan. So my work as an amateur sleuth made a beginning.

That glimpse of the names Houghton and Hesketh coming together in a family tree reminded me of a document described by Sir Edmund Chambers, and later more fully discussed by the late Oliver Baker in *Shakespeare's Warwickshire and the Unknown Years* (Simpkin Marshall, 1937). This document was the last will and testament, dated 3 August, 1581, of Alexander Houghton, a gentleman of considerable property, who resided at Lea Hall, near the River Ribble, by Preston in Lancashire.

The passage in this will that caught Chamber's eye, and later excited Baker, was the following:

> Yt is my mind and wyll that Thomas Houghton of Brynescoules my brother shall haue all my Instrumentes belonginge to mewsyckes and all maner of playe clothes yf he be minded to keppe and doe keppe players. And yf he wyll not keppe and manteyne playeres then yt ys my wyll that Sir Thomas Heskethe Knyghte shall haue the same Instrumentes and playe clothes. And I most hertelye requyre the said Sir Thomas to be

ffrendlye unto ffoke Gyllome and William Shakeshafte nowe dwellynge with me and eyther to take theym vnto his Servyce or els to helpe theym to some good master as my tryste ys he wyll.

Evidently these Lancashire worthies, Houghtons and Heskeths, were in the habit of keeping 'playeres'. Just what this meant, exactly what was the activity and employment of these 'playeres', is a question that leads us far into interesting fields.

English dramatic records are full of complexity; yet through them one can trace the development of our theatre of today from the early Miracle play, Morality and 'Enterlude', on to the less crude and more realistic comedy, which led in turn to the euphuistic operative plays of Lyly and the melodramas of Kyd, Marlowe, Greene and Peele.

The records are ancient, and in the domestic papers of old families, in municipal and churchwarden's accounts, in diaries and all kinds of documents, we find reference to players, their entertainment and payment for performances in mansion, college, guildhall and moot-hall.

In the Middle Ages players were hospitably received at the monasteries and priories. Durham Abbey can, for example, exhibit in its Account Rolls, many entries of payments to players, minstrels, jesters, harpers and the like, and often the names of their patrons – King, Queen or nobleman, whose men they were – are given. In the Transactions of the Surtees Society, vol. 100, p. 503, we find a record of the year 1300, when 'hystrioni Regis', 'the King's players', were rewarded with twelve pence. A much later entry of 1579 tells us that 26s. 8d. was 'given to the earle of Lecesters players'.

Of minstrels it is perhaps interesting to find in the Towneley papers a record that Robert Nowell of Read Hall, close to Martholme, the seat of our Sir Thomas Hesketh, also of Rufford, paid in July 1569: 'To James Shr. Thoms heskethe minstrell' twelve pence.

The sixteenth century was the age of the galleried inns, set around quadrangular courtyards, where the strolling players and tumblers gave their performances. These tiered galleries accommodated the spectators and formed an ideal auditorium from which to witness the diversions presented in the courtyard below. From the inns of Tudor England may be traced the principle upon which the playhouses of Shakespeare's London were built – the first theatres known as the Swan, the Rose, and of course the immortal Globe: 'this wooden O.'

Who were these players who called at mansion, guildhall and inn? One can make a resounding list of the noblemen under whose protection the various troupes of players ranged the country, often appearing in London at Court and at the earlier theatres there, such as the Curtain. Each player wore the badge of his patron upon his sleeve, and their manager who travelled with them was well provided with credentials or licence which he would produce to any county officials who might raise objections to the players exercising their talents within their township or parish. For it must be remembered that in those days, and indeed until their Royal recognition by James I, actors were considered, at any

PLATE III

SIR THOMAS HESKETH, KT. (1539-87) OF RUFFORD, LANCS.
From the Pedigree Roll in the Department of Manuscripts at the British Museum (B.M., Add. MS. 44026). Reproduced by permission of the Trustees.

PLATE IV

HENRY STANLEY, K.G., FOURTH EARL OF DERBY (1531-93).
From the original portrait in the possession of R. Cunliffe Shaw, Esq., F.R.C.S., F.R. Hist. S.

rate within the strict meaning of the Laws, to be classed with 'rogues and vagabonds'!

Sir Edmund Chambers, in his lectures at Oxford between 1929 and 1938, gave a clear analysis of the relationship between player and patron in the public and private theatre of Shakespeare's time. The members of an acting company were linked together in two ways. First, they had a business agreement among themselves, known as a 'composition'. Each member gave a bond to carry out its terms, contributed to the stock of property (for which he was repaid on retirement), and had a right to share in the takings, which were divided at frequent intervals. Not all of these, however, went to the players; some – entrance fees to galleries – were set aside for the rent paid to the owners of the playhouse, who might be either outside capitalists, or an inner ring of the better-off members of the company, sometimes known as housekeepers. All this appears from contemporary lawsuits; players, like many other Elizabethans, were litigious folk.

There is no composition surviving for any of Shakespeare's companies; but there are records of the shares he held in the Globe and the Blackfriars. These are not specified in his will; but we do not know when, or to whom, he parted with them.

The other unifying link in each company was its 'lord', or 'patron'. Every company had one; in the case of a London company, the patron was generally some nobleman prominent at Court. In a sense the players were his household servants. They wore his livery and badge; they apparently did not receive wages from him, but if they performed before him they would get a 'reward'. Usually, however, they were able to play for their own profit in the theatres, or on country tours; and on these, their allegiance to their lord protected them. They carried with them his letter of recommendation, and in Shakespeare's time also a licence from an officer of the Royal household known as the Master of the Revels.

An amusing sidelight on the career and ambition of a typical player is given in an anonymous pamphlet of 1605, *Ratseis Ghost*. This concerns the merry life of one Gamaliel Ratsey, a Northamptonshire highwayman; one chapter describes 'a pretty prancke passed by Ratsey upon certaine Players that he met by chance in an Inne'. Disguised, Ratsey asks the players to give him a 'private play', and rewards them liberally; the next day he pursues them professionally, and forces them to return his forty shillings, with interest. Then he benignly advises their leader to quit the provinces and make his fortune in London:

> Get thee to London, for if one man were dead, they will have much need of such a one as thou art. My conceipt is such of thee, that I durst venture all the money in my purse on thy head to play Hamlet with him for a wager. There thou shalt learne to be frugall – for players were never so thriftie as they are now about London – and to feed upon all men, to let none feed upon thee; . . . and when thou feelest thy purse well-lined, buy thee some place or lordship in the country, that, growing weary of playing, thy monie may

there bring thee to dignitie and reputation; then thou needest care for no man, nor not for them that before made thee prowd with speaking their words upon the stage . . . and in this presage and propheticall humour of mine, says Ratsey, kneel down – rise up, Sir Simon Two Shares and a Half; thou art now one of my knights, and the first knight that ever was a player in England.

The 'one man' who played Hamlet must be Burbage; the 'frugall' reference may well be to Alleyn, who in the year of the pamphlet retired with a comfortable fortune largely earned from speaking Shakespeare's words upon the London stage. Or it may equally be to Shakespeare himself, whose industry and thrift enabled him to buy New Place in 1597.

Shakespeare was helped towards his gains by a notable company of players, formed from the amalgamation of two patrons' troupes – a brave show of talent to bring a flood of silver into the paybox of the Globe. He had belonged to the troupe known as Strange's Men, under the patronage of Ferdinando, son and heir of the Earl of Derby; the Earl had no private company of his own, although he was a notable patron of players, enjoying regular theatrical performances at his houses of Knowsley and Lathom. Ferdinando succeeded to the Earldom soon after the Earl of Leicester's death, following which he joined his company to that of Leicester; the augmented troupe became known as Derby's Men; and later still, the Chamberlain's Men. As we shall see, Strange's Men had probably previously been joined by Sir Thomas Hesketh's Players, who possibly included a young man called William Shakeshafte.

Most of the Companies bore distinguished names: Lord Robert Dudley's (Leicester's Men), Sir Robert Lane's, Lord Clinton's, the Earl of Warwick's, the Lord Chamberlain's, the Earl of Essex's, the Queen's, the Lord Admiral's, the Earl of Pembroke's the Earl of Worcester's. There were others; and beyond these, many private troupes kept by provincial squires and knights, from which local talent was absorbed into the great companies.

The Derby houses, especially Knowsley, seem to have provided a stage for many dramatic presentations. Chambers writes: 'the travels of the Queen's Men of 1588 were prolonged until the end of that year, and extended as far north as Lancashire, where they were at the Earl of Derby's house of New Park on October 16.' For 1590, in which year the Company's main provincial visits are undated, he conjectures a summer tour, by Ipswich to Norwich (April 22), then perhaps by Leicester and Nottingham to Knowsley (June 25-6), where 'Mr Dutton' (one of two brothers, both actors, known as the 'chameleon' Duttons from their practice of often changing companies) was again a visitor, thence through Shrewsbury (July 24), Bridgnorth and Ludlow, and home by Coventry and Oxford.

Lord Strange's Company between the years 1580 and 1587 was merely a troupe of acrobats or tumblers composed of boys or youths. In the provincial records they are mentioned at times as 'Lord Strange's tumblers', 'Symons and his fellowes', and as 'John Symonds and Mr Standleyes Boyes' –

THE ANNOTATOR

Strange's name being Ferdinando Stanley. As from 1588 the change of designation is confusing, and Professor Harrison[1] notes chronologically the titles this company bore from time to time, as follows:

1588. On the death of the great Earl of Leicester the best actors of Leicester's and Strange's apparently reorganised into a new 'Lord Strange's Company'.

1592. Strange's Men acted for a time at the Rose and afterwards travelled under the leadership of Edward Alleyn. (STRANGE'S)

1593. (25 Sept.) Lord Strange became Earl of Derby. (DERBY'S)

1594. (16 April) The Earl died. His players now took service under Henry Carey, Lord Chamberlain. (CHAMBERLAIN'S)

1596. (23 July) The Lord Chamberlain died and the players were taken over by his son George Carey, Lord Hunsdon.
(HUNSDON'S)

1597. (17 March) Lord Hunsdon became Lord Chamberlain. (CHAMBERLAIN'S)

1603. (17 May) James I became patron of the Company. (THE KING'S MEN)

Strange's father, the fourth Earl, was a friend of Leicester; hence the transfer of Leicester's Men to the service of Strange in 1588. This transfer brought into the company the players Augustine Phillips, Thomas Pope, George Bryan, William Kemp,

[1] *Shakespeare's Fellows* (John Lane, 1923)

THE ANNOTATOR

Richard Cowley, Richard Burbage, John Heminges, Henry Condell, William Sly, John Duke, Christopher Beeston, and for a while Edward Alleyn. These were Shakespeare's fellows – and more; two names stand out to deserve the gratitude of all who speak English. It was John Heminges and Henry Condell who, seven years after Shakespeare's death, gathered and edited for posterity the edition of his *Comedies, Histories, & Tragedies* which we know as the First Folio.

So much for these companies of players, with which in their northern castles and mansions, far from the glitter of the Court and the diversions of the Bankside playhouses, the nobility and gentry were wont to lighten the tedium of winter evenings in music and masques. So much for the background of Houghton's and Hesketh's players. My random and roaming search for some clue, some prompting name, that might help me to the identity of that attentive reader of Richard Newport's book, seemed to have led me far afield. Like Oliver Baker, I had felt something more than a twinge of curiosity about that oddly-sounding William Shakeshafte; and I wanted to follow his tracks.

V

Proud of employment, willingly I go.
(LOVE'S LABOUR'S LOST, 2.1.35)

ALEXANDER HOUGHTON, the master of William Shakeshafte, lived at Lea Old Hall, a mansion standing on the north shore of the Ribble estuary. Near it the Salwick Brook makes a diminutive estuary of its own, and at high tide serves as a moat on that side of the house.

'As seen from the highway,' writes Oliver Baker,[1] 'it promises no sign of antiquity, but on the side towards the Ribble its tall elevation is much more interesting. There it is easy to recognise that the ornamental timbers of an oak-framed manor-house such as are more perfectly preserved in fine old Lancashire mansions and especially at Rufford, have here at Lea been almost entirely replaced by Queen Anne or Georgian brickwork.

'At the eaves the medieval coving of plaster and oak ribs is still in position undisturbed, and has below it a very massive wall-plate beam carved with the billet moulding, but these are the only external features of the original house remaining.

'Within, there are several rooms on the ground floor in which finely moulded oak posts can be seen which reach from the ground to the roof. There are also shapely beams supporting the ceilings. On the first floor the same moulded uprights are again

[1] *Shakespeare's Warwickshire and the Unknown Years*

visible, and at the end of the building one can, by ascending to an attic, see the massive timbers of the first great truss of a series, which formed an elaborate roof to what must have been originally a very noble great chamber.'

There the venerable Elizabethan, Alexander Houghton, sat at meat with his household; there his players gave diversion.

Alexander died soon after the execution of his will, which was proved on 12 September 1581. Shakeshafte and Gyllome would then presumably have entered the service of Thomas Houghton, taking with them the bonus of a whole year's wages generously left them by his brother. (He also left an unusual sort of pensions scheme, based on a sweepstake system, for certain of his household, including the two young men.) However, Thomas Houghton (third son of Sir Richard Houghton, and in fact only a younger half-brother to Alexander), was slain in a fray at Lea in 1589, and moreover there is no indication that he was ever 'minded to keppe', or did keep, players. So Sir Thomas Hesketh seemed the next subject for investigation.

In the British Museum Department of Manuscripts, with the splendid Pedigree of the Heskeths, illuminated on vellum, before me, I settled to enjoy the quaint portrait of the old gentleman himself and that of his wife 'Dame Alice one of the daughters to Sir John Holcrofte Knight'. Sir Thomas, for all his damascened armour, chained across the plated breast, is all the benevolent squire, with bald pate and forked grey beard. Warrior he had been, however – witness the account written in a border below the Pedigree: 'This Syr Thomas Heskaithe knight serued his souvraigne in Scotland and at the Seigh of Leethe and theare was sore hurte in diverse places and had his ensigns strooken doune which hee had recouered again with greate commendacione for his forwardines seruice. And was in his latter dayes a noteable great housekeeper and Benefactor to all men singular in euery science and greatlie repaired the house at Martholme and Homes wood and the chappell at Rufford.' A later chronicler, Raines, tells us of his Knighthood the day after the coronation of Queen Mary, October 2nd 1553, and of his captaincy of a hundred men raised by him to serve his Queen in the Scots wars. He was Sheriff of Lancashire in 1563, and was in confinement as a disaffected papist in 1581.

Sir Thomas had two favourite houses; Martholme, the Manor House of Great Harwood, and Rufford Hall, both in Lancashire. The first is now a farm, its once proud gate-house an untended ruin; but Rufford Hall, by Ormskirk, to which William Shakeshafte was directed by the will of Houghton, is almost as it was in Henry VII's day. The Great Hall is described by Barbara Freeman in *Open to View* (Benn, 1952).

> The interior of the Great Hall has a rude magnificence unsuspected from outside. The great hammer-beams bear angels holding shields, and the plaster between them is thickly patterned with crossing beams. Two oak trees worked to an octagonal shape form the sides of the great arch at the East end. Between them stands a unique

survival, the massive 'movable' screen. Lively Gothic carvings enrich its panels, heavy framing and ponderous base. It is topped by three fantastic spires, possibly late Jacobean in date, and like nothing so much as grotesque Oriental headdresses.

Sir Thomas was well-connected among the great families of Lancashire, Cheshire and Shropshire, and an ancient shield of stained glass in the window of a bay in the Hall at Rufford bears the arms of the Stanleys, Earls of Derby and Kings of Man.

I could at first find no direct evidence that Sir Thomas ever kept players.

However, a fortuitous discovery was brought to my attention, one that suggested that at any rate the 'instrumentes belonging to mewsyckes' found their way from Lea Hall to Rufford. Shortly after I reached this stage in my quest, Lord Hesketh found at his home, Easton Neston, some old musical instruments which were among household effects moved some years previously from Rufford. These may well be some of those catalogued in an inventory, now in the County Records at Preston, of the goods of 'Robert Hesketh late of Rufforth' at 16 November 1620. The list of instruments includes 'vyolls, vyolentes, virginalls, sagbutts, howboies and cornetts, cithron, flute and taber pypes'. An assortment that would have well suited a small stage orchestra.

One other recorded item confirms that Sir Thomas did in fact maintain a company of players, which Shakeshafte and Gyllome would presumably have joined. The Household Books of the fourth Earl of

THE ANNOTATOR

Derby, Strange's father, included a register of the guests who visited the Earl at his houses in Lancashire between 1586 and 1590. They were kept by the Earl's Steward or Comptroller, William Farington (of whom we shall have more to say). On 30 December 1587, he noted at Knowsley, 'On Saturday Sr. Tho. hesketh plaiers went awaie.'

This entry was misread by Canon Raines, who first transcribed it for the Chetham Society in 1853; a flaw or blotch in the paper made it appear to read, 'Sr. Tho. hesketh, plaiers went awaie.'

This supposed comma, since ascertained by others beside myself to be unauthentic, misled searchers along these tracks. Nevertheless, the Houghton will, transcribed by the Rev. G. J. Piccope in *Lancashire and Cheshire Wills* for the Chetham Society, 1860, was noticed by Chambers in 1923, and aroused Oliver Baker's excitement in 1937, when he discussed the possibility of 'Shakeshafte' being Shakespeare; and Sir Edmund Chambers expanded the point in *Shakespearian Gleanings* (Oxford University Press, 1944):

> It is clear that if William Shakeshafte passed from the service of Alexander Houghton into that of either Thomas Houghton or Sir Thomas Hesketh, he might very easily have gone into that of Lord Strange, and so later into the London theatrical world, where we find in 1592 William Shakespeare, writing probably for Lord Pembroke's men, and called by the envious Robert Greene 'the only Shake-scene in a countrey'.

I did not seem to be getting any closer to confirming the identity of our annotator; but I seemed to be getting caught in the fringes of that old conundrum that has ensnared so many literary enthusiasts – the problem of Shakespeare's 'hidden years'.

VI

*In seeking tales and informations
Against this man . . .*
         (HENRY VIII, 5.3.110)

IN the quest of a further trace of Shakeshafte, Lancashire was evidently the most likely covert to draw. Sure enough, before I had gone far, I came across an odd fact, insubstantial and unimportant enough in itself, which nevertheless offered a coincidence that fell into position with the satisfying clink of a precision-made part. It fell into place, that is, in a chain of ideas regarding this Shakeshafte which – with no logical justification, and despite discouragement from my more cautious instincts – had been linking itself up in my mind.

In the summer of 1950 I had motored up to Rufford with Geoffrey Brown, who has been a close ally in much of my quest. The magnificence of the Hall was set off by velvet lawns and foliage glowing in golden sunlight. Philip Ashcroft, the founder of the Folk Museum at the Hall, showed us the beauties of the place, and then took us in to tea. There have been Ashcrofts of his branch in Rufford since the fourteenth century.

I confided in him the nature of my own search; and then he told me that there had been for a very long time in the peaceful village of Rufford, the oral tradition that William Shakespeare had been at the Hall as a young man.

This was said of many other old manor houses in every part of England, I ventured. Ashcroft told us that his mother had the tale from her father, Lawrence Alty; and that Alty, who can have had no special motive or inclination for fabricating such a tale, was born in Rufford in 1837.

In Alty's day, no link between Shakespeare and Rufford had been recorded; but this, I now remembered, was no longer true. During his recent investigation[1] of Shakespeare's friends and intimates, Professor Leslie Hotson touched on that very Shakeshafte, our own elusive quarry. In his fascinating essay Professor Hotson pointed out, with regard to Chambers' suggestion that Shakeshafte might be Shakespeare in all but name, that 'it clearly does not make Sir Edmund's conjectural identification look less interesting' when we find that Shakespeare, taking part in a deal of shares of the ground-lease of the Globe in 1599, had as one of his chosen fellow-trustees a man born in Rufford.

Thomas Savage, born about 1552, died in 1611 in comfortable prosperity earned as a sea-coal measurer of London, and a member of the Goldsmith's Company, and also from property dealing and owning; wherein, Professor Hotson points out, he was concerned with John Heminges. In his will he bequeathed forty shillings to the poor of 'Rufforthe, where I was borne', and twenty shillings

---

[1] 'John Jackson and Thomas Savage', in *Shakespeare's Sonnets Dated* (Hart-Davis).

THE ANNOTATOR

to his cousin, the widow of Thomas Hesketh of Rufford.

It was to him that Shakespeare and three of his fellows chose to entrust their half-share in the ground-lease; and I noted with lively interest that the man chosen to accompany him in this trust, was that William Leveson whom we have already observed as kin to the Newports and their Shropshire circles.

However, no further light seemed to offer itself along the line of Savage's tracks; as Professor Hotson says, it seems 'an astonishing coincidence and no more'. Related by marriage to the Thomas Hesketh to whom William Shakeshafte was commended; acquainted with players of the Lord Chamberlain's Company; and chosen to be a partner in a negotiation of which William Shakespeare was a prime mover. Born, also, in a village which, though many hundred miles from London or the 'Shakespeare country', nevertheless believed itself once to have sheltered the poet.

Pondering on Savage, I remembered that another of Shakespeare's fellows was thought to have had a Lancashire origin: Edward Alleyn, born in London in 1566, who travelled in 1592 with Strange's Men, and was for a time their leader; and later in life, the Founder of Dulwich College. Of him, W. H. Blanch recorded that his mother was Margaret Towneley, daughter of John Towneley, of Towneley in Lancashire. 'Documents at Dulwich College seem to give evidence that Mrs Alleyn was married a second time to a person of the name of Brown, an actor, and it was owing to this circumstance, doubtless, that young Alleyn was (according to Fuller in his *Worthies*) "bred a stage-player".'

The Towneleys, incidentally, had some slight connexion with the Houghtons through a marriage in the time of Alexander Houghton's grandfather.

Following up Edward Alleyn's Lancashire tracks, I next came to his inclusion among the notabilities to whom a volume of Epigrams was dedicated in 1599. J. M. Nosworthy, Lecturer in English in the University of Wales, put me on the track of John Weever, who, I found, retired ungraduated from his sizarship at Queens' in 1598, and returned to his Lancashire home. A year later he published his *Epigrammes*, written two or three years before.

Weever, I was glad to discover, seems to have been well acquainted with the Lancashire circles we are beginning to know. Alleyn, to be sure, has an epigram to himself; but the whole work is dedicated to a Houghton – Sir Richard, High Sheriff of the County, and nephew of Alexander Houghton. Another verse is dedicated to Sir Thomas Holcroft; his aunt Alice married Sir Thomas Hesketh of Rufford – familiar names! – but we shall find ourselves, in the course of this tangled pursuit, running often across Holcrofts: one married a Fitton (and was mother of the 'Dark Lady'); another an Earl of Rutland; another chain of family connexions runs Holcroft – Fitton – Leveson – Sheldon – Throckmorton – Arden. At the beginning of the *Epigrammes* there are complimentary verses by another Holcroft; and the 22nd Epigram is addressed 'Ad Gulielmum Shakespeare'. A later work of Weever's, *Faunus and Melliflora* (1600) is dedicated to Edward Stanley; it has commendatory verses by M.D. (who is Drayton); R. H. (who might be Richard Houghton); I.F. (possibly a Fitton); and T. H. (who might be Thomas Holcroft).

In the introductory stanzas to the *Epigrammes*, Weever says that he wrote most of them when he was only twenty, speaks of his Cambridge education, and confesses that he is ignorant of London. In the sonnet addressed to Shakespeare, he extols the poet's early works – his narrative poems and historical plays: and he mentions as well-known characters,

> Romeo, Richard; more whose names I know not.

'Richard' is more likely to refer to *Richard III*, probably written in 1592, than to the later *Richard II*. It occurred to me that some light might be thrown on my search if I could trace any record of an early Lancashire performance of *Richard III*.

Where could such a record be found? Probably, in the confused and unexplored state of so much of English private archives, only by chance. However, the performance need not necessarily have been in a private house; it is known that there was in Elizabethan days a public playhouse at Prescot (a fact that came to me one day when Sharpe France, County Archivist of Lancashire, dropped in at the Gate House).[1] Prescot is barely two miles from Knowsley, the seat of the Earl of Derby, and would have been a convenient port of lucrative call for

---

[1] *Transactions of the Historical Society of Lancashire and Cheshire*, Vol. CIII, p. 69

any of the companies who had been to act at Knowsley, when no longer required by their patrons; and would have been a natural opening date for Strange's Men setting out on their provincial tours.

Prescot is about ten miles from Warrington; and Warrington was the home of Euphemia Carill. I don't know who she was, or where W. Carew Hazlitt, who introduced her to me in his *Shakespeare; The Man and his Work* (Quaritch, 1912), met her; but it is my private suspicion that she was taken to see an early performance of the first version of *Love's Labour's Lost*, given by Strange's Men in the Prescot Playhouse even as early as 1587.

My suspicions arose from the following. Robert Tofte wrote in 1598, in *Alba: The Months Minde of a Melancholy Lover*,

> Loues Labour Lost, I once did see a Play
> Yclepèd so, so callèd to my paine,
> Which I to heare to my small Ioy did stay,
> Giuing attendance on my froward Dame ...

and with regard to this obscure allusion (which is pointed out by the Cambridge editors, and has been much milled over) Hazlitt writes:

> ... But the mention in a printed book of 1598 (i.e. *Alba* ...) of the visit of Robert Tofte to the exhibition of *Love's Labour's Lost*, then a recent play, which he had seen on its original appearance some time before, in company with his mistress, Euphemia Carill, of Warrington, has a bearing of its own, although the writer – Tofte himself – tantalises us in a not unusual way by keeping strict

silence as to what he thought of the piece and the author, and as to the nature of the cast. All that he deemed it necessary to say was that the title and the texture of the drama caused him pain, and that he stayed at the house reluctantly in attendance upon the lady. Tofte by no means stood alone in failing to foresee that posterity would have been in an immeasurably greater degree his debtor, had he at any rate supplemented the expression of his transient personal sentiments with a ray or so of light on the scene under his eyes.

Somehow I felt that my Saturday morning chasing Robert Tofte had not been entirely useless; yet clearly, as with Weever and *Richard III*, some definite evidence of an early Lancashire performance of *Love's Labour's Lost* is what one hopes will eventually come to light – possibly a record of that early staging which is mooted by the Cambridge editors: 'In our opinion its first performance had Christmas 1593 for date and for place some great private house.'[1] This, they suggest, would have been a production of an earlier version of the play, drafted well before 1598, the date of the Quarto, 'newly corrected and augmented by W. Shakespere', of this 'Pleasant Conceited Comedie'.

The play is full of obscure and undoubtedly topical allusions, which have caused endless head-scratching to all editors. Now, taken in conjunction with our Lancashire hints and hazards and echoes, it seems to me that two of these allusions may give us new levers to prise open the secret. First,

[1] *Love's Labour's Lost*, New Cambridge edition, p. xii

the 'School of Night' allusion (4.3.140, and the whole 'skit' of the Academe of Navarre); secondly, the parodied 'pageant of the nine Worthies', in 5.2.

Professor Dover Wilson and Dr Frances Yates have independently examined the jesting at the 'School of Night', with what Dr Yates calls its mockery of high-flown intellectual pretensions, as a reply to Chapman's obscure poem *The Shadow of Night*, published in 1594. We are told by Dr Yates (*A Study of Love's Labour's Lost*, Cambridge University Press, 1936) that 'the studious young men in the play can be interpreted as representing either the Raleigh group, immersed in their studies, or the Essex-Southampton group who laugh at schemes of that kind. Chapman lets us know who some of Raleigh's friends were in his dedication to the *Shadow of Night*, where he mentions the Earl of Derby (known as Lord Strange before coming into the title), Lord Hunsdon, and the Earl of Northumberland, as being amongst those who pursue knowledge with proper seriousness. Efforts have been made to connect Derby with the King of Navarre in the play through his Christian name, which was Ferdinand, and through some punning on the word "strange".'

The connexion might well lie at one remove. Professor George Connes, in *The Shakespeare Mystery* (Palmer, 1927) draws attention to William Stanley, sixth Earl of Derby (in fact Connes jestingly plays the devil's advocate and offers him the crown of Shakespeare!).

William Stanley was born in 1561, younger son of the fourth Earl, whose heir was Ferdinando, Lord

Strange. Like him, William went to St. John's College, Oxford, in 1572; and in 1582 at the age of twenty-one he began his travels in France in the charge of a Welsh tutor, Richard Lloyd. In Paris William was received at the Court of Henry III, to whom his father was deputed in 1584 to confer the Order of the Garter. Afterwards he visited the Loire, Orleans, Blois, Tours, Saumur, Angers; then we lose trace of him, but Connes conjectures that Stanley was in Navarre between 1582 and 1587. Stanley and his tutor Lloyd were back in England and at Lathom House, the other great Stanley mansion, in June 1587, when a great cycle of theatrical representations was given there, lasting more than a month; the Earl of Leicester's company played the chief part in the performances. (This was the company that, on the death of Leicester, was merged into the service of Strange. It included actors who became the fellows of William Shakespeare – Phillips, Pope, Bryan, Kemp, Cowley, Burbage, Heminges, Condell, Sly, Duke, Beeston, Cook and, for a while, Alleyn.)

Evidently the 'School of Night' allusion is not likely to have been written into the play before 1594. It is in some way a riposte to Chapman's *The Shadow of Night*, dedicated to Roydon in 1594. This refers to the academic-astronomical movement started by Northumberland and others, as being of recent development:

> But I stay this spleen when I remember my good Matthew, how joyfully oftentimes you reported unto me that most ingenious Derby, deep-searching Northumberland, and skill-embracing

Earl of Hunsdon had most profitably entertained learning in themselves to the vital warmth of freezing Science . . .

Peele's allusions to the movement in his dedication to the *Honour of the Garter*, which is dated 26 June 1593, are as follows:

Renowned Lord, Northumberland's fair flower,
The Muses' love, patron and favourite,
That artisans and scholars dost embrace.
And clothest Mathesis in rich ornaments,
That admirable mathematic skill,
Familiar with the stars and Zodiac,
To whom the heaven lies open as her book;
By whose directions undeceivable,
Leaving our Schoolmen's vulgar trodden paths,
And following the ancient reverent steps
Of Trismegistus and Pythagoras
Through uncouth ways and unaccessible,
Doth pass into the pleasant spacious fields
Of divine science and philosophy . . .

However, there are many reasons for dating the play even earlier than this. Arthur Acheson[1] argues that it was originally written in 1591, revised in 1594-5, after Shakespeare had read *The Shadow of Night*, and 'corrected and augmented' again in 1598. The germ of the play may, I feel, derive from some even earlier show.

Connes (with his tongue in his cheek) speculates that at the Court of Navarre, William Stanley and Lloyd 'found a number of Protestant gentlemen. The period of three years, during which time, in

---

[1] *Shakespeare's Lost Years in London* (Quaritch, 1920)

Love's Labour's Lost, the men pledge themselves to renounce women's society, corresponds to the duration at first assigned to his travels.' At Stanley's return in 1587, a play of this kind might well have provided a fitting 'masque of homecoming', the material of it gleaned from and decorated by the returned travellers' tales; bringing in a graceful compliment to the elder brother Ferdinando, as the King of Navarre.

The play includes a mock 'pageant of nine Worthies' and that would also have brought a topical touch to the occasion. William Stanley's tutor Richard Lloyd was a dull pedant and a pompous pedagogue; not unlike Holofernes – with whom, no doubt, after his tours with his noble charge through France and Italy, he would vie in larding his conversation with 'O.K.-phrases' in European tongues. More germanely to the issue (I am indebted to Professor Abel Lefranc and Dr A. W. Titherley for drawing my attention to this) Lloyd published in London in 1584, under R. Warde's imprint, 'A briefe discourse of the most renownded actes and right valiant conquests of those puisant Princes called the Nine Worthies'. These nine were Joshua, Hector, David, Alexander, Judas Maccabaeus, Julius Caesar, Arthur, Charlemagne, and Guy of Warwick. Lloyd's book was an approximate transcript of the annual Chester pageant, which included a show of the nine worthies, followed by the seasons – two of which appear in *Love's Labour's Lost* as singers. But there is a striking resemblance between Lloyd's handling and introduction of the Worthies and that in the play, where only five actually appear (as the pageant is interrupted). The wording is often an obvious skit, e.g.,

> *Lloyd:* A Lyon wich sitting in a chaire bent a battel-axe in his paw argent.
> *Love's Labour's Lost:* Your lion that holds his poll-axe sitting on a close-stool.

Lloyd's pedantry has been transformed into clever burlesque. It would not have been entirely unflattering for him to have his work alluded to, even satirically; and might have made some amends for the cruel portrait of him in the pedagogue Holofernes.

Let us toy a moment with the fancy that in June 1587 Leicester's Men wanted an improvised 'number' for a spare evening at Lathom. William Shakeshafte was at hand with Hesketh's players, Rufford Old Hall being only a short distance away. He offered them a lightly-drawn, hastily-composed play of topicalities. A few years later, William Shakespeare found this early exercise a convenient frame in which to hang his 'School of Night' skit; and later still rounded it out again for 'Her Highnes' and the Quarto.

Ay me, I fondly dream! Let us get back to some facts: facts about Shakespeare's Lancashire acquaintances, and any traces of local colour that appear in his plays.

VII

Then, there is the County Palatine ...
(MERCHANT OF VENICE, 1.2.49)

My remaining facts about Shakespeare and Lancashire fall into no obvious sequence or pattern, but each one seems to add weight to our slender framework of conjecture and coincidence.

Fact One. A copy of Chaucer's Works recently sold had been in the possession of two 'Elizabethan Poets, Robert Tofte and Sir George Buc'. Before that, its owner (probably the first) had been Margaret Radcliffe of Ordsall, Lancashire. The Radcliffes were noted as visitors to Knowsley by Farington in his household book. Margaret's brother Sir Alexander Radcliffe was a friend of the Earl of Essex, and died in battle in Ireland in 1599. Soon after, Margaret died of a broken heart, and her death was the subject of a touching epitaph by Ben Jonson.

Fact Two. Margaret was one of Elizabeth's Maids of Honour, together with Mary Fitton of Gawsworth, Cheshire, and Elizabeth Vernon of Hodnet, Shropshire, a cousin of Essex and of Shakespeare, and the bride of Shakespeare's patron Southampton; all names well known in the Knowsley circles. These Northern maids and their gallants evidently enjoyed a private joke, now somewhat obscure, which had a Shakespearian foundation. Professor

Hotson[1] recently found among the uncalendared papers at the Public Record Office a note from Essex to Sir Robert Cecil, dated 25-28 February 1598, carrying this postscript:

> I pray you commend me also to Alex Radcliff and tell him for newes his sister is maryed to Sr. Io. Falstaff.

Margaret in fact never married. Professor Hotson suspects a jibe at the susceptibilities of Henry Brooke, Lord Cobham, an enemy of Essex, who had made Shakespeare change the family name of 'Oldcastle' in *Henry IV* to the immortal one of Falstaff, and whose notorious lechery ill became his grey hairs.

The joke was revived by Elizabeth Vernon in a letter of 1599, now among the Cecil Papers, to her husband Southampton.

> Al the nues I can send you that I thinke wil make you mery is that I reade in a letter from London that Sir John Falstaf is by his M(rs) Dame Pintpot made father of a godly milers thum (a boye thats all heade and veri litel body). But this is a secrit.

Sir Edmund Chambers thinks that this again was a tilt at Lord Cobham, notoriously childless, for all his pestering of young women.

Fact Three. Another Radcliffe, Robert, second Lord Fitzwater, an earlier collateral of Margaret's family, took the side of Henry VIII against Catharine of Aragon and was rewarded with the Earldom of Sussex. His second wife was Margaret Stanley,

---

[1] *Shakespeare's Sonnets Dated*

daughter of the second Earl of Derby. Now I quote from F. E. Halliday's *Shakespeare Companion* (Duckworth, 1952).

Sussex's Men. Thomas Radcliffe, 3rd Earl of Sussex, became Lord Chamberlain in 1572, in which year the company first appeared at Court, and then fairly regularly until his death in 1583. They are sometimes called the Chamberlain's during this period. The year 1583 saw the formation of the favoured Queen's Company, and under the patronage of Henry, 4th Earl, they disappear from the Court records until January 1592. His son Robert became 5th Earl in December 1593, during the plague year when all the companies had to travel. However, they played for Henslowe at the beginning of 1594, in a repertory of twelve plays, one of which was 'titus & ondronicous', Q1 of *Titus Andronicus* being published that year as having been 'Plaide by the Right Honourable the Earle of Darbie, Earle of Pembroke, and Earle of Sussex their Seruants'. In April 'the queenes men and my lord of Sussex together' gave eight performances at Henslowe's theatre. Perhaps they joined the Queen's for they are not heard of again as an independent company until 1602, after which they are traceable in the provinces for many years. It is possible that the 4th Earl was the 'Lord' for whose company Kyd and Marlowe were writing in 1593, and also that Shakespeare wrote *Titus Andronicus* for them.

Where did they pick up *Titus Andronicus*?
What, asks Dover Wilson (New Cambridge Edition, xlviii), was Shakespeare doing at the

beginning of 1594 with the Earl of Sussex's Men, a company not otherwise associated with his name? How did a play written by Peele for the Strange-Derby troupe, come into possession of this other company, and then a few months later pass into that of the Lord Chamberlain's men with whom Shakespeare acted, and for whom he wrote for the next twenty years? A possible answer to all this is that Sussex's men bought the play in the first instance, engaged Shakespeare to enlarge it, and, going bankrupt, as it seems they did immediately after, had nothing to give him in return for his labour except the prompt-book resulting from it. Such an answer would explain how *Titus* became part of the Chamberlain's men's repertory, and would also explain the rather surprisingly early entry of the play in the Stationers' Register on the last day of its performance by Sussex's company.

Critical opinion has held (Dover Wilson disagrees) that *Titus Andronicus* appeared on the stage, in some form in 1591 or earlier. Steevens discovered the reference to it in the anonymous *A Knack to Know a Knave*, played by Strange's Men in June 1592:

> As Titus was vnto the Roman Senators
> When he had made a conquest on the Goths.

This has been cited to support the earlier date, as has the entry in Henslowe's register of the Strange's Men season at the Rose in 1591, of 'ne tittus & vespacia', i.e. a new play. Halliday observes:

> The title suggests a play about the destruction of Jerusalem by Vespasian and his son Titus, but Strange's had a play of *Jerusalem* in their 1592

Rose repertoire; if it were about Titus and Vespasian, it is quite possible that Henslowe muddled his title, and by *Titus and Vespasian* meant *Titus Andronicus*. This is made more probable by the fact that Lucius, Titus Andronicus's eldest son, who revenges his injuries, is called Vespasianus in a German version printed in 1620. There is a MS note, probably of the Revels office, *c.* 1619, which includes four of Shakespeare's plays and *Titus and Vespasian*. On the whole it seems probable that by 'tittus & vespacia' Henslowe meant *Titus Andronicus*, though it may not have been new in the strict sense. . . .

Dover Wilson, in his introduction to the New Cambridge *Titus Andronicus* sets aside this conjecture that 'Henslowe muddled his title', by reconsideration of two other allusions to *Titus and Vespasian* in the anonymous *A Knack to Know a Knave.* 'Manifestly, we have as much right to assume these lines refer to a play as we have in the case of those which Steevens cites; more in fact. For, though neither passage, taken by itself, proves anything more than that the writer of *A Knack* was familiar with a story or two about the Titus or Vespasian of whom he speaks, the seven performances by Strange's company of *Titus and Vespasian*, recorded by Henslowe during the two months preceding the first production of *A Knack*, make it pretty certain that the allusions to Vespasian are to this play in the repertory of the same company, and already well known on the stage.'

The case for an independent lost play of *Titus and Vespasian*, belonging to Strange's Men, is strengthened by the fact that from the library at Knowsley there was recently sold a fifteenth century manuscript on vellum; an English poem in rhymed couplets on *Titus and Vespasian, or the Destruction of Jerusalem*. This anonymous poem, probably composed in the middle of the fourteenth century, has as its theme the capture of Jerusalem by Vespasian and Titus, regarded as the supreme act of God's vengeance on the Jews for the death of His Son. The poem was first printed in 1905, as a Roxburghe volume, edited by A. J. Herbert, based on a fifteenth century manuscript in the British Museum;[1] the Knowsley MS. was unknown to him and therefore not recorded.

If this small volume was in the library at Knowsley in the sixteenth century (as it may have been), it could surely have been the source of inspiration for the *Titus and Vespasian* of Strange's Men? Resident 'university pens' must have had access to their patron's bookshelves. Shakespeare, incidentally, was evidently familiar with the theme:

> Do like the mutines of Jerusalem,
> Be friends awhile and both conjointly bend
> Your sharpest deeds of malice on this town.
> (*King John*, 2.1)

Though the existence of this lost play would dispose of one reason for holding to the earlier date of *Titus Andronicus*, there is one allusion in the play which makes me feel that it must have been in existence, in some form, earlier than 1593.

In 1589, the new company at Knowsley formed by the fusion of the best players of Strange's and

---

[1] Add. MS. 36523

Leicester's would be looking round for plays worthy of them, whether brand-new or old refurbished. They would find with them a bright and willing, and studious, man of about twenty-five, recently joined after the death of Sir Thomas Hesketh and the dissolution of his troupe. He could have been put to work, either helping Peele to get out a 'rush job', or polishing up a confused prompt-book of the previous year.

It might have been at his suggestion, or just because all the company had been hearing Ballads in the Lancashire ale-houses, that a horrible scene, reminiscent of a local tradition, was incorporated.

I came across it first in Elliott O'Donnell's *Haunted Britain* (I am an omnivorous reader of ghost stories and legends). Radcliffe Tower in Lancashire, is supposed to be haunted by a black dog, the spirit of a wicked woman who caused the murder of her stepdaughter, 'Fair Ellen of Radcliffe' and had her flesh made into a pie for her father to eat. This is how it is told in the ballad:[1]

> Now when his lord he did come home
>   For to sit down and eat,
> He callèd for his daughter dear
>   To come and carve his meat.
>
> 'Now sit you down', his lady say'd,
>   'Oh sit you down to meat;
> Into some nunnery she is gone,
>   Your daughter dear forget.'

[1] *Lady Isabella's Tragedy or the Stepmother's Cruelty;* a black-letter broadside in the Pepys Collection, printed in Percy's *Reliques;* also in *Ballads and Songs of Lancashire* (Harland and Wilkinson)

Then solemnly he made a vow
  Before the companie,
That he would neither eat nor drink
  Until he her did see.
Oh then bespake the scullion-boy,
  With a loud voice so hye—
'If now you will your daughter see,
  My lord, cut up that pye.
Wherein her flesh is mincèd small,
  And parchèd with the fire;
All caused by her stepmother,
  Who did her death desire. . . .'

The reader will recall 5.3 of *Titus*, and the hero's mad revenge upon Tamora, whose sons Chiron and Demetrius had mutilated and ravished his daughter Lavinia. Titus, assisted by the stricken Lavinia, cut the throats of the culprits and made a pie of their heads. At the banquet to Tamora and her consort Saturninus, after they have eaten the pie, Titus kills Lavinia and declares the authors of her outrage. 'Go,' says Saturninus, 'fetch them hither to us presently.'

Titus: Why, there they are both, baked in this pie,
  Whereof their mother daintily hath fed
  Eating the flesh that she herself hath bred.

The Radcliffe – Sussex's Men – Radcliffe Tower coincidence seems too remote to have significance; yet it is possible to imagine that the Radcliffe family legend, and its disguised appearance in *Titus Andronicus*, may have roused Sussex's Men's interest in the play.

A conceit in Act 4 scene 3 of the same play sent me off into new dreams.

THE ANNOTATOR

Before the palace in Rome
Enter Titus, Old Marcus, his son Publius, young Lucius, and other gentlemen, with bows; and Titus bears arrows with letters on the ends of them.

Titus and his kinsmen are met together to indulge in fanciful archery, and he declares that since there's no justice on earth,

> We will solicit heaven, and move the gods
> To send down justice for to wreak our wrongs.
> Come, to this gear. You are a good archer, Marcus
>
> (*he gives them the arrows, according to the superscription on the letters*)

Titus: 'Ad Jovem', that's for you: here, 'Ad Apollinem';
'Ad Martem' that's for myself:
Here, boy, to Pallas; here, to Mercury:
To Saturn, Caius, not to Saturnine;
You were as good to shoot against the wind.
To it, boy! Marcus, loose when I bid.
Of my word, I have written to effect;
There's not a god left unsolicited.

Marcus: Kinsmen, shoot all your shafts into the court:
We will afflict the emperor in his pride.

Titus: Now, masters, draw. (*They shoot.*) O, well said, Lucius!
Good boy, in Virgo's lap; give it to Pallas.

Marcus: My lord, I aimed a mile beyond the moon;
Your letter is with Jupiter by this.

Titus: Ha, ha!
Publius, Publius, what hast thou done!
See, see, thou hast shot off one of Taurus' horns.

Marcus: This was the sport, my lord: when Publius shot,
The bull being galled, gave Aries such a knock
That down fell both the Ram's horns in the court,
And who should find them but the empress' villain?
She laughed, and told the Moor he should not choose
But give them to his master for a present.
Titus: Why, there it goes! God give his lordship joy!

Suddenly there came to me the whole scene of a performance of *Titus* in the great Hall of Derby's house at Lathom, and the players of his heir Lord Strange with their bows and arrows; the dialogue ringing, as each player shot his letter-bearing arrow over a great screen painted with the signs of the zodiac. For such a screen was a permanent and conspicuous feature of the hall at Lathom where the 'plaiers plaid'. Strange's mother, the Countess Margaret, was interested in astrology as well as sorcery (she and her husband the Earl were friends of Dr John Dee of Manchester) and Parker, her Yeoman of the Wardrobe, who was a student of astronomy, designed for her this zodiacal screen or planetarium, which Chaloner described in an obscure laudatory poem of 1576.[1] It served to indicate the diurnal changes of sun, moon and planets. Very possibly Chaloner himself executed Parker's design for the Countess: that Thomas Chaloner of Chester, mentioned above in chapter I. He was a

---

[1] Chetham Soc. Stanley Papers, Part I

freeman of Chester in 1584, and died on 14 May 1598.

Dover Wilson finds traces of original Shakespeare in this scene, as well as of Peele, and even of the 'old style' of Kyd. And we know that Shakespeare was fond of archery – or at any rate, of allusions to it.

> In my school-days, when I had lost one shaft,
> I shot his fellow of the selfsame flight
> The selfsame way with more advised watch,
> To find the other forth; and by advent'ring both,
> I oft found both: I urge this childhood proof,
> Because what follows is pure innocence.
> I owe you much; and, like a wilful youth,
> That which I owe is lost: but if you please
> To shoot another arrow that self way
> Which you did shoot the first, I do not doubt,
> As I will watch the aim, or to find both,
> Or bring your latter hazard back again,
> And thankfully rest debtor for the first.

It would, I mused, be nice to think of the young Shakespeare, on leaving home to be a singing-boy with Alexander Houghton at Lea Hall, 'losing one shaft' by adopting his grandfather's variant-surname of Shakeshafte and 'shooting his fellow of the selfsame flight' (a 'shaft') towards the goal of ambition, to win back the 'speare' of maturity and fame. But one can speculate on theories like these until the cows come home! At least we can be agreed that the poet was fond of toxophilic word-play.

Ending this chapter, which I admit has contained matters of contention and speculation mingled with things indisputable, I must add two more facts which connect Shakespeare with Lancashire: they both have to do with Knowsley.

In August 1587, William Farington entered in the Household Book: 'On Saterday Mr Salusbury and his wieffe and unkell came.' This couple departed on 28 August; and towards Christmas came again: 'Dec. 15. Mr Skaresbrike came and also Mr Salesbury.' Canon Raines, the learned editor of the reprint of the *Derby Household Book*, identified Salusbury as John, later Sir John, Salisbury of Lleweni, Co. Denbigh, on the Welsh border. He succeeded to the family estate in 1586, and a few months later married Ursula Stanley, natural daughter of Henry, fourth Earl of Derby.

Salisbury, himself a poet, kept open house to men of letters, especially local bards. Among these was Robert Chester, a retainer of his. In 1601 Chester published a volume of verse entitled *Love's Martyr*, to celebrate the knighthood of his patron, and to this Shakespeare contributed an enigmatic poem, *The Phoenix and Turtle*.

I found it something more than amusing to reckon, that when John Salisbury came to Knowsley visiting his father-in-law in December 1587, Sir Thomas Hesketh's players were there too. It seems likely that they included in their number one William Shakeshafte. So it is not impossible that during that Christmas visit there began a friendship between a rising young poet and a Welsh squire, which was later to be marked by a somewhat cryptic contribution from an established playwright to a complimentary volume in honour of a neighbour. (For Salisbury left his

Welsh estate in 1595 to enter the Inner Temple.)

Another visitor to Knowsley often noted by Farington, was one 'Hamlet Holcroft'; possibly a relation of Alice Holcroft, Thomas Hesketh's wife. Possibly a relation too, of a certain Captain Holcroft, one of the Cecil intelligence corps, who sent home many confidential reports on the siege of Ostend in 1601 (preserved at Hatfield). 'Particularly interesting', writes Chambers, are the 'numerous advices' concerning the Siege of Ostend; and he points out that this siege was almost certainly the original of 'the little patch of ground' alluded to in *Hamlet*, 4.4.

VIII

That youth is surely in this company.
(AS YOU LIKE IT, 2.2.16)

WILLIAM SHAKESPEARE has given us many a picture of many a life, but unhappily not a word about his own – a most vexatious man! Had he left but a bundle of letters or even half a diary we should be well content to settle into our stalls and enjoy his plays without caring a button for his identity. But we know so little about him, we may even at moments doubt whether he wrote his own plays – particularly if we fall in with Baconians, Oxfordians, or other heretics to confound and dismay us.

Thinking about all the facts and clues, hints and coincidences, that I had stumbled over in my pursuit of a thoroughly elusive annotator, I began to wonder if one might not build up a new pattern for the 'hidden years', springing from that mention of 'Shakeshafte'; going on, in fact, from Oliver Baker's hypothesis:

> In stating that the poet may have found a home with a band of Players in Lancashire and passed the most impressionable years of his life in great houses, and with cultured people, instead of remaining in a butcher's yard till he married and left for London, I may not have provided the reading public with the sort of detailed narrative of Shakespeare's early life and work which we

should all like to read, but it is one which puts less strain on their credulity than what has sometimes been offered them, and is at least less insulting to their intelligence.[1]

Why 'Shakeshafte'? Why, in the first place, this name which as far as we know, the playwright never used, nor was called by?

First, it must be remembered that there was in those days a far greater flexibility in surnames than we can now easily imagine. Shakespeare's grandfather Richard lived at Snitterfield, Warwickshire. In the parish records he figures indifferently as both Shakeschafte and Shakespeare. Shakeshafte was also a common Lancashire name, far commoner than Shakespeare (Sharpe France told me he had found sixty of them in Lancashire). A young man who was anxious to fit in with the household, or who wished to be unobtrusive for other reasons, could easily have adopted the local variant. It is even possible that the lawyer executing Houghton's will, or his scrivener, would have set down 'Shakeshafte' as the more usual form of the name 'Shakespeare'. Certainly when Robin Greene in 1592 jibed at 'the only Shake-scene in a countrey', this third mutation of the name misled nobody.

Next, why so far afield as Lancashire?

It is known that John Shakespeare, William's father, was at one time highly regarded in Stratford and held municipal offices, but later fell into trouble which became so grave that in 1580 he was summoned before the Court of Queen's Bench. It is

[1] *Shakespeare's Warwickshire and the Unknown Years*

not clear exactly what led to this, but 'from the legal expressions employed, taken in conjunction with the circumstances of the time, we may believe that adherence to Catholicism would adequately explain the affair'. John Semple Smart, in *Shakespeare Truth and Tradition* (Arnold, 1928), considers the question thus, and goes on to explain:

> By the middle of Elizabeth's reign the resolute Catholics who were ready to endure all things for their cause had become a small and harried minority; but there were still many waverers who accepted the new faith with reluctance. . . .
> No clear-cut distinction had yet been drawn between Catholic and Protestant; and many men who were willing to accept the Sovereign as head of the Church still clung with affection to the old rites with which they had been familiar from childhood. . . . On several occasions, when the extreme Catholics themselves had plunged into dangerous and treasonable practices, the work of repression was carried on with peculiar energy and comprehensiveness. One of these outbursts of severity took place in 1580.

John Shakespeare's name twice appears in lists of men at Stratford who clung to the 'Old Religion' and would not attend parish church: – 'recusants'. It seems very probable that if, in the middle 1570's, he was becoming unpopular in Stratford and being harried for his faith, he would have felt that the town grammar school was no place for his son to be brought up in. 'There were', writes Professor Dover Wilson in *The Essential Shakespeare*, 'excellent alternatives . . . which would be fitter nurseries for dramatic genius and more in keeping with that passion for music which we know Shakespeare possessed. If, for example, he received his education in the service of some great Catholic nobleman it would help to explain how he became an actor, since the transition from singing-boy to stage-player was almost as inevitable at that period as the breaking of the male voice in adolescence.'

Now Alexander Houghton of Lea Hall was a Protestant; one of his brothers was a Catholic exile, and his wife Elizabeth was also definitely Catholic. It was evidently she who had the say in these matters, for after her husband's death she was reported to the Commissioners as harbouring at Lea 'an obstinate Papist well acquainted with seminaries, and he was teaching the children to sing and plaie upon the virginalls'.

Alexander's elder brother Thomas was a staunch Romanist; and we shall see later how he may well have been known in Stratford-on-Avon.

Apart from that, we do not know what recommendations John Shakespeare may have been able to find to help his son into patronage at Lea Hall as a singing-boy. What little we do know of the boy should have been helpful. Canon Raines in 1836 put paid to the tradition, started by Aubrey, that William Shakespeare had been a butcher's boy, who 'when he killed a calfe . . . would doe it in a high style, and make a speech'. Raines pointed to the old dramatic representation of *Killing the Calf* and asked: 'Was this the calf that Shakespeare killed?'

Of course it was. Far easier to believe in than the

butcher's shop service, is the notion that the youthful William was skilled in the pseudo-ventriloquial diversion of throwing his voice into the dummy head of a calf pushed through a curtain, as he must often have seen done by strolling players in the town where he spent his childhood. In the years when his father was High Bailiff of Stratford, William Shakespeare would certainly have been familiar with players; in those years there is record of visits by Chamberlain's, Worcester's, and Warwick's companies. John Shakespeare would have been among the dignitaries responsible for receiving the Players. (Later, in 1587, no fewer than six companies seem to have visited the town in a single season.)

The performance of 'Killing the Calf' was merely a comedy 'turn'. A clown would indulge in crosstalk with the dummy head pushed through the curtain. When the calf's head became too glib for the interrogator, the clown seized a broadsword of wood and struck off the head, which tumbled on to the stage. In *Hamlet*, 3.2 we find Shakespeare's own allusion to the 'turn' so popular in his youth:

HAMLET (*to Polonius*): My lord, you play'd once i' th' university you say?

POLONIUS: That did I, my lord; and was accounted a good actor.

HAMLET: And what did you enact?

POLONIUS: I did enact Julius Caesar: I was kill'd i' th' Capital; Brutus kill'd me.

HAMLET: It was a brute part of him to kill so capital a calf there. Be the players ready?

Another possible allusion may be found in

Nashe's preface to Greene's *Menaphon*, 1589, where their rival player-poet is cited among 'the alchemists of eloquence, who (mounted on the stage of arrogance) think to outbrave better pens with the swelling bombast of bragging blank verse, indeed it may be the ingrafted overflow of some *killcow* conceit'.

It may be supposed that it was the young William Shakespeare's skill in this crude mimicry, together with other musical leanings, that helped his father to find him his new employment. Once safely installed at Lea Hall, he evidently made good progress, for three years later, when his employer died, he singled him out, not only for special commendation in his will, but also for the unusual legacy of a year's wages. Thus provided, it would not be surprising if the young man sped home to the town beside the Avon, for a holiday before moving on to his new employment.

Whether or not he stayed at home longer than he intended, we know that he found trouble there, and in the following November (1582) married Anne Hathaway, not before it was time. There he seems to have stayed awhile; Susannah was born in May following. Perhaps country contentments and paternity appealed to him then, and perhaps a gentle job in his father's glove-shop took care of board and lodging. Before long, however, the twins arrived, Judith and Hamnet – this latter name, Hamnet or Hamlet, it is to be noted, was a common name in Lancashire at the time. Now we can well believe that both domestic cares, and the need for money, may have urged the player afield again;

and now he may have taken himself to that Sir Thomas Hesketh of Rufford to whom his earlier patron had commended him.

If he needed further introduction to Rufford, it would have been possible for him to have found that locally also. Worcester's Men visited Stratford in 1582; with them, probably that year and certainly the next year, came the sixteen-year-old Edward Alleyn. We remember that Alleyn was 'bred a player', and that his mother was a Towneley of Lancashire, and a relative of the Heskeths. If Shakespeare, feeling the weight of being a young father, shared gossip and 'shop' and ale with the visiting players of an evening, and so struck up acquaintance with the boy Alleyn, the friendship may have proved a useful one.

Whenever he eventually did turn to Rufford, there he would have found a thoroughly Catholic household – one marked by Lord Burleigh on his map of prominent recusants. At one time indeed Sir Thomas Hesketh was imprisoned in Manchester Castle, under the wardenship of Sir Edmund Trafford and Robert Worsley,[1] along with other recusants. Another pointer to the religion observed at the Old Hall is the recently-disclosed 'Priest's Hole' in the gable-end of the Hall, with its aperture placed to overlook the Stations of the Cross carved on a nearby roof-spandrel.

From Rufford, ambition, or a taste for the glamour of a great noble household, or simply love of good company, or even an interest in play-acting, would have brought the youth more and

---

[1] Alwin Thaler, *Faire Em in Lancashire*

more into the Knowsley circles. And as far as religion was concerned, there he would have found a tolerant moderation. Derby was one of the Ecclesiastical Commissioners against recusancy; but showed no fiery zeal in his office.

Shakespeare's hypothetical progress might be dated as follows:—1578, or earlier: John Shakespeare's money or religious troubles had begun, and he sent the fourteen-year-old William to Lea. Towards the end of 1581, the ex-singing boy received an extra year's wages and returned to Stratford. 1582, marriage to Anne Hathaway. 1585, to Rufford to join the Hesketh Players.

Three years after this date, Sir Thomas Hesketh died, and his players were in all likelihood absorbed into Strange's Men. If Shakespeare went with them, and was already wearing the mark of coming greatness, there may well have been sown at this time the seeds of jealousy in another playwright, which later flowered in an open attack. Greene had been courting the favour of the Derbys since 1584, dedicating *The Myrrour of Modestie* to the Countess in that year; but by the time he published *Menaphon* and *Ciceronis Amor* (dedicated to Ferdinando Strange), his territory was already being invaded, not by other University wits, its previous sole lords, but by an 'upstart crow' of a provincial player. At the end of the few bitter and penurious years left to him, in 1592 the dying Greene dipped his quill in gall and penned a last sneer at the 'absolute *Iohannes fac totum*, in his own conceit the only Shake-scene in a countrey'.

After that date, 1592, we move among known

facts and charted landmarks. Greene's sneer in *A Groatsworth of Wit* warned his fellow dramatists against a successful actor-playwright, now evidently established in London. Then the publication of *Venus and Adonis* in 1593, and *Lucrece* in 1594, both dedicated to the young and influential Earl of Southampton, showed that Shakespeare had safely reached shelter under the wing of friends at Court.

In the forefront of his new achievements was to come the cycle of the York and Lancaster history plays: a theme very likely to fascinate a youth spending impressionable years at Rufford, where he could peruse many coats of arms of related families in the painted glass of the oriel window – the Eagle and Child of Stanley prominent among them.

For an ambitious young actor-writer employed at Knowsley, work on a series of plays which would give good opportunity for flattering his masters and their influential friends would no doubt seem attractive. These would be plays which would gratify his Lancastrian audience by magnifying the deeds of their noble forebears; the prospect of work on such a series might well tickle ambition as well as intellectual fancy.

William Shakespeare, we know, started his dramatic exercise on the history plays with work on *Henry VI*. Dover Wilson calls *Part I* of the trilogy 'richer in military incident and poorer in poetry than any other play in the cycle'. In time, it did not necessarily come first of the three parts; it (or another play of the same name) was acted by

Strange's Men at the Rose in March 1592; but many of its allusions were topical to the late summer and autumn of 1591, and it may have had its first performance in that year. Much of the play is ascribed generally to Shakespeare; all of it by Professor Peter Alexander. But as Dover Wilson writes,[1]

> 'A topical play asks haste, since national excitements are at all times short-lived . . . and haste in play-making is most readily secured by setting a team of playwrights to work. . . .'

So it seems probable that in the middle of 1591 Shakespeare was turned to patch, mend and polish for Strange's Men, some sections of a rough version or synopsis of a play (Dover Wilson thinks it may all have been 'plotted' by Greene) – an eminently suitable job for a quick, intelligent, and industrious, though not academically learned, young man attached to the Derby household.

Before *Part I*, he may already have worked over *Parts II* and *III*, which are thought by Dover Wilson and others to be earlier. In these two plays, Stanleys figure at various points. The most notable instance – and the one most likely to attract favourable attention from a Stanley audience – comes at 4.5.23 of *Part III*, where King Edward singles out Sir William

---

[1] *New Cambridge Shakespeare. Henry VI Part I*, xxi

It may have been a risky way of getting a play; but whoever made the plan had a sharp sense of 'box office', as we know from Nashe's famous entry in *Pierce Pennilesse* (1592):

'How it would have ioyed braue Talbot (the terror of the French) to thinke that after he had lyne two hundred yeares in his Tombe, hee should triumphe againe on the stage, and haue his bones embalmed with the teares of ten thousand spectators at least (at seuerall times) . . .'

Stanley, one of his rescuers, for a special promise of reward (a point not suggested by the Chroniclers). In *Part II*, it is a John Stanley who conducts the Duchess of Gloucester prisoner to the Isle of Man.

It is, however, in the sequel, *Richard III*, that this partiality to the Stanleys shows most clearly. Chambers calls this play 'a masterpiece from the same hand which contributed, to how small or great an extent it is impossible to tell, but in any case prentice-wise, to the final shaping of those typical dramas of a pre-Shakespearian epoch, the three parts of *Henry the Sixth*'. As I pointed out in chapter VI, an early performance of *Richard III* at the Prescot playhouse, by Strange's Men as they set out on tour from Knowsley, might neatly account for John Weever's memory of the play.

In *Richard III*, Thomas Stanley is the prime mover in that action which ends in the triumph of the house of Lancaster-Tudor over the house of York; he exercises a deterrent influence on King Richard, intervenes efficaciously on several occasions (not mentioned by Holinshed), and finally when he deserts Richard for Richmond, who becomes King Henry VII, Shakespeare strives to make the treason sympathetic.[1] It is Stanley who puts the crown on the new King's head; it is Stanley who goes to escort the Queen to the coronation at Westminster (another point not owed to Holinshed).

This Thomas Stanley is called 'Derby' by the playwright (e.g. 1.3) as well as 'Stanley' (e.g. 4.2). The two titles are used almost in alternation through

---

[1] I am indebted for these points to Professor Georges Connes, *The Shakespeare Mystery*

PLATE V

FERDINANDO STANLEY, LORD STRANGE, LATER FIFTH EARL OF DERBY (1559-1594). *From the original portrait in the possession of Eric B. Porter, Esq.*

PLATE VI

WILLIAM FARINGTON (1537-1610) OF WORDEN, LANCASHIRE, STEWARD TO HENRY, FOURTH EARL OF DERBY. *From the original portrait in the possession of R. Sharpe France, Esq., F.S.A. (see Appendix v, A Model for Malvolio).*

the play; though in fact the Earldom of Derby was not given to the family until later, after the victory of Bosworth. Shakespeare was evidently not averse to reminding his hearers that Thomas Stanley was a direct ancestor to, and bore the same names as, Henry fourth Earl of Derby and his son Ferdinando; and that the rise of these great patrons of players and playwrights was closely connected with the rise of the Tudors and the achievements of Henry VII, Ferdinando's great-grandfather. A young man of genius, finding himself in intimate acquaintance with this Northern aristocracy, at Rufford and Knowsley and Lathom, would have been well-placed to obtain 'inside information' on family history, and to put his own particular stamp upon that which he learned outside the chronicles; and would perhaps not have worried if strict accuracy were sometimes to seek.

A further connexion of the Stanleys with the history plays must now be explored; it is a conjunction heralding more omens across our northern sky.

I have already touched on the subject of John Shakespeare's 'old religion', and the theory that his leanings to recusancy may have urged him to arrange that his son's education should be developed among the remoter Catholic households of Lancashire rather than at the town school of Stratford, where, as he already knew too well, anti-Catholicism was vigorous.

The Heskeths and Houghtons held to Rome; but

the attitude in the Stanley household appears to have been more non-committal – Derby seems to have executed his duties as Ecclesiastical Commissioner with laudable moderation. Most probably the Stanleys' religious position was much what Shakespeare's seems from his plays to have become: an awareness of both sides of the question, an acceptance of the new regime without rancour against the old, with no inward urge to crusade for either; in fact, an essentially *English*, tolerant and unfanatical point of view.

As the Derbys were not outspokenly anti-Romanist, it is understandable that a group of Roman Catholic gentlemen in exile should have thought that Ferdinando Lord Derby might listen to their seditious blandishments, and set himself at their head as Pretender to the Throne; maintaining the right derived from his mother, Margaret Clifford, a granddaughter of Henry VIII's sister the Duchess of Suffolk. They so far misjudged their man that the plot broke on his loyalty; and one of its principals, Richard Hesketh, a son of Sir Thomas, was taken and executed in 1593. Soon after the plot, Ferdinando died; poisoned, it has been suggested. His younger brother William, who became sixth Earl, has been suspected of having a hand in his death. How far this is true, and how far William was involved in the sedition, is a question whose answer may well have been buried for ever in the ruins of Lathom, the second great Derby house, which was razed to the ground during the Civil War.

The Derbys' right to the Throne was much canvassed by Catholics, and in 1594 a manifesto was published at Antwerp setting out the whole theory of the question.

A Conference about the next Succession to the Crown of England, divided into two Parts. Whereunto is added a New and Perfect Arbor or Genealogy of all the Kings and Princes of England from the Conquest unto this day: whereby each man's pretence is made more plain.

This appeared under the name of Doleman: but according to Connes (*op. cit.*), it was in fact written by the Jesuit Robert Parsons, in collaboration with Cardinal Allen and Fr. Englefield. It affirms the right of the House of Lancaster, descending from John of Gaunt; asserts the legality of deposing bad kings, such as Richard II; and plumps for William Stanley as the most proper successor to the Throne.

Professor Connes points out that this Catholic manifesto analyses exactly those questions of succession with which Shakespeare was concerned in the History Plays, and from much the same viewpoint. It seems to me probable that these high questions first engaged Shakespeare's mind when he was a member of the Stanley household, and still a close neighbour of those Catholic circles among whom he had previously lived. A young man intent on incorporating family history into his own dramatic chronicles of the struggle for the Throne, would have been fascinated by a new echo of the dispute, of urgent topicality in the family of his patron. And perhaps his thoughts on this question might have later found expression, or at any rate reflection, in his plays about the Right of Kings.

IX

*. . . I have been
The book of his good acts*
(CORIOLANUS, 5.2.15)

At this point we seemed to have provided a rough, hypothetical answer to the question, where was Shakespeare, if and when he made these notes? Lea, Stratford, Rufford, or Knowsley. But what other independent reason had we for supposing that the *Chronicle* had been to any of those places? It looked as if I might still sadly have to look out an answer to that alternative query, who was the annotator if *not* Shakespeare, and where was he when he made his notes?

It seemed possible that his spelling might give some clue to his background. Yet a fair description of its chief tendencies and characteristics came most easily to hand in Fripp's *Shakespeare Man and Artist* (O.U.P., 1938) where he describes the typical orthography of Warwickshire men and Midlanders in Shakespeare's day.

> Spelling was phonetic, and not, as we are sometimes told, chaotic. Those who could write, including scholars, spelled according to sound, and no two men, even in the same town, spelled quite alike; nevertheless, every educated man had his standard of pronunciation and was more or less consistent in his spelling. . . . Peculiarities of

spelling as of writing, are more marked than inconsistencies.

What was the English of these worthies? How did they pronounce and spell? Their speech was nearer to that of Chaucer than to that of Doctor Johnson: closer to the Saxon, the Norman and the Latin. . . . A multitude of words were in use among Shakespeare's Warwickshire contemporaries . . . which would sound French and un-English to Johnson and very foreign to us.

For instance, they said *auncient, chaunce, counsaile, daunger, inchaunt, marvaile, slaunder, sodaine, straunge, vertue*, and so forth. But they loved their old English *aunswer, blewe, emonges, togyther, uppe, ynough*. . . . They added weight to terms of both native and foreign origin, by supplementing *g* with a *d* – *alledge, lardge, liedge, priviledge; ch* with a *t*, as in *atcheeve, ritch; k* with a hard *c*, or vice versa, *druncke, suncke, wrinckle*. . . . They clung to the old initial *Y*, as *Yedward, yearth*. They lingered moreover on their consonants, especially in words of one syllable, doubling them in the spelling – *Godde, madde, sinne, wille;* lingered on their long vowels in monosyllables, preferring *y* to *i* in spelling – *vyne, ryse, tyme, wyde* . . . and were not too busy to say and write *fairnesse, heathennesse, wantonnesse*.

Other forms of pronunciation and orthography which, if not universal, were widespread in the Poet's country, must be noted. The Chaucerian final *e* was no longer sounded: but *ye* with its dainty vocal *e* was replaced by *ie* rather than the bald *y*, as in *busie, privie, studie, wittie*. The initial *y* for *i* is common – *ydle, ynne, yron*. The adjectival *ious* is more popular than *eous* – *couragious, out-*

ragious. The initial *in* is much more in favour than *en*, as in *incompass, incounter, intertainment*.

(And Fripp intersperses many more examples, and gives derivations.)

It will be seen that this gives a fair description of many of A.'s spelling habits, as the reader can judge from Appendix ii; though it does not account for those two favourite tricks of his, past participles ending *yd* ('regardyd', etc.) and present participles ending *inge* ('approchinge', etc.), nor for the Latinity of such words as *discention, reservation, historiographier*.

Well, if he was a 'provincial', could he have got at the book at or near its original home in Shropshire? Did Shakespeare ever go to Shropshire? There is, as a matter of fact, some reason to suppose that he did, whether it was to annotate this book or not. As we have seen, if he was well known to Heskeths and Houghtons, and in touch with their kin, stretching to Herberts and Newports, it would not have been difficult for him to get introductions to that part of the world. Perhaps he held an appointment as tutor there in those supposedly Stratford years, 1581-5, which might have provided the grain of truth for Beeston's 'in his younger yeares a schoolmaster in the countrey'; perhaps he returned there for a later spell when the theatres were closed during a plague.

The idea of a sojourn in Shropshire is supported by the many Shropshire allusions in the plays, from Falstaff's 'long hour by Shrewsbury clock' (put up, incidentally, in 1595) to the 'dancing horse', alluded to in *Love's Labour's Lost;* this apparently was the great sensation of Shrewsbury in 1591. My wife once made a list of one hundred and two Shropshire words that appear in the plays. A curious point is that the name 'Estridge' was borne by a hill to the north of the Vesson in the parish of Habberley, and was there known to be a name for a species of large falcon.[1]

> All furnished, all in arms,
> All plumed like estridges that wing the wind . . .

Further Shropshire coincidences will be found in Appendix viii.

To approach the question of whereabouts from the other end, where was the *Chronicle* when A. (or Shakespeare) made the notes?

For a clue to this, we must now return to the remaining item of *external* evidence, the pressmark **EEd**.

For ten years this mark of ownership, though by its combination of letters it told of shelf-room in a considerable library, resisted all efforts at identification. One man offered to sell me the secret for fifty guineas, but turned out to be disinclined to put up reasonable guarantees. The label had been pasted inside the upper cover of the *Chronicle* when it was rebound, probably at the end of the seventeenth or early eighteenth century. Marks of such a large and recent library ought to be easy to find: but they have not been.

Chance eventually brought me the clue. One winter evening early in 1953 I was working with C. K. Ogden on the selection and cataloguing of

---

[1] Rev. C. H. Drinkwater, *Transactions of Shropshire Archaeological Society*, February 1885

the books which were to go from his library to University College, London. It must have been nearly midnight when, happening to turn over the cover of a calf-bound seventeenth-century folio, I caught a glimpse of a little label bearing the letters **App**.

'That', said Ogden, 'looks very like your "EEd" in Halle.'

And indeed it did. The book was *The Theory of the Earth*, London, 1691; and the label was identical in typeface and character with my 'EEd'. Moreover, beneath it there lay a late seventeenth-century signature, *'Robert Worsley'*.

This is certainly little enough to go on; the signature is earlier than the label, and there is no reason to suppose that the *Chronicle* always lay in the same library as *The Theory of the Earth*. But at any rate there was equally no reason to suppose the contrary: in pitch darkness the faintest gleam is worth pursuing. So I resolved that night to work on the hypothesis that towards the end of the seventeenth century the *Chronicle* belonged to Robert Worsley, whoever he may have been.

I had bought the book in 1940 from a Yorkshire house, where it lay among a dump of uncatalogued books; in this case, in a bundle with a dilapidated Bible and an equally dilapidated dictionary, with the auction slip of the previous sale still tucked in one of the volumes. The owner could give me no information about the previous sale, or the origin of the dumped books; nor could the many local booksellers I consulted. But the likelihood was that the former sale had not been far afield: and consequently, quite apart from its annotations, I had always been on the lookout for some explanation of the book's presence in Yorkshire – or in nearby Lancashire.

When I woke up the morning after our discovery of **App**, I found that Worsley had become intertwined with Knowsley in my mind. Reaching for Raines' edition of the *Derby Household Books*, I found in Farington's diary for 19 August 1587: 'On Sonday a greate company: on Monday my L. rode to Lathom, wch daye Mr Salusburye and his wiffe, Mr Halsall & Mrs Dorothie, & also Mrs Franses & *Mr Worseley*: on Tuesday my L. rode into Wirrall, Mr Salusbury & his wiffe to Sefton, on wch daye all strandgers went away.' Canon Raines identifies 'Mr Worseley' as being Thomas, son of 'Robert Worsley of Booths Esq.', a considerable landowner in Lancashire, and one of the magistrates who distinguished himself by his zeal against the recusants, wherefore he was appointed a Warden of the New Fleet Prison in Manchester, where, I remembered, he at one time held in not unfriendly custody Sir Thomas Hesketh of Rufford.

It seemed very probable that the *Chronicle* had lain in the possession of a descendant of his, a later Robert Worsley, at Hovington, Yorkshire, where Thomas Worsley settled. This Robert would have been the great-great-grandson of the Manchester Warden; the Derby, Salisbury, Hesketh, acquaintanceship of his forebear seemed to suggest a number of ways by which the book might have come into his possession.

However, I believe that in those days possessions

moved about more often through family links than in any other way, so I decided to look for any possible family connexion between Richard Newport of High Ercall and Robert Worsley of Booths.

I found one – a remote one, through two marriages – but one that provided the oddest and firmest click of coincidence of almost any that we have heard in this strange eventful history.

Robert Worsley married Elizabeth, second daughter of Sir Thomas Gerard of Bryn. Her sister Catherine was wife of Thomas Houghton, the Romanist elder brother of Alexander Houghton of Lea. The link between Newport and Houghton we know. (See Appendix i.)

So if the *Chronicle* travelled along the family chain, it looks as if it would have sojourned at Lea Hall when Alexander Houghton's brother was master there. And there a little later, as we have said, we believe that the youthful Shakespeare was a favoured member of the household.

X

*. . . Nor read the subtle-shining secrecies
Writ in the glossy margents of such books.*
(RAPE OF LUCRECE)

*And what obscured in this fair volume lies,
Find written in the margent of his eyes.*
(ROMEO AND JULIET, I.3)

SHAKESPEARE was evidently accustomed to the idea of notes and glosses in the 'margents'; very possibly he was in the habit of making them himself. Now I believe that these notes in the margin of Halle were made by Shakespeare, in his early days, probably before he was twenty. What then emerges? What can we learn about him?

Among the possible deductions, one point immediately stands clear: Shakespeare's youthful sympathies were predominantly Roman Catholic; he would seem to have been educated in that faith. This in its turn would lend weight to our theory that his father, in trouble as a recusant, sent him away from Stratford to enjoy the more desirable background of a household with Romanist sympathies; and so on round the mulberry bush.

Among the recusant supporters of the old faith, there were other possible connexions between Stratford and the Lancashire gentry; these now seem worth looking into. I am grateful to Miss Diana Neill for leading me to my first clue along the following track:

THE ANNOTATOR

Simon Hunt, an M.A. of Oxford, who was nominated by the Earl of Warwick as master of Stratford Grammar School and licensed in that post in 1571, turned his sympathies towards the persecuted English Romanists in 1573; a time when presumably he had Shakespeare under his tuition. His pupils expressed their 'mislike' of this papistry by smashing the school windows. Two years later Hunt left for Douay in France, where he matriculated with other *Angli pauperes* in July 1575, and where he finished his days as an instructor.

Douay was an English college for Roman Catholics, which survived in France until the French Revolution. When its safety was threatened by political disturbances in the Netherlands, its members used to be divided between Rome and Reims; and it was at one period, 1578-94, when the principal house was established at Reims, that the organisation attained its highest celebrity.

The Overseas College of Douay was founded in 1568 by Cardinal William Allen, who later had the help of Thomas Houghton, elder brother of the Alexander Houghton who has played a part in our tale. It is a strange fact that Alexander's younger half-brother 'of Brynescoules,' was also named Thomas. The elder Thomas's story is thus given by *The Bibliographical Dictionary of English Catholics*:

> On the death of his father (Sir Richard), Thomas Houghton succeeded to his extensive estates. Some few years previously he had married Catherine, daughter of Sir Thomas Gerard of Bryn, and had a son, Thomas, and a daughter Jane, born about 1557, who became the wife of

James Bradshaigh, of The Haigh, Esquire. Between the years 1563 and 1565 Thomas Houghton replaced the old manor house at Houghton Bottoms by the imposing erection which still rears its majestic towers on the summit of Houghton Hill. At this period William Allen, afterwards Cardinal, visited Lancashire, and was a guest at Houghton Tower. In common with the gentry and people of Lancashire Houghton repudiated the new religion which was being forced upon the country . . .

. . . Under these circumstances, feeling that he could not remain in the country and keep his conscience, Houghton took the advice of his friend Vivian Haydock, and in 1569 or the beginning of the following year, he hired a vessel and sailed from his mansion of The Lea (Lea Old Hall) on the Ribble, to the coast of France, and thence proceeded to Antwerp. For this he was declared an outlaw and possession taken of his estates. On March 17, 1576, his half-brother Richard, ancestor of the Houghtons of Park Hall in Charnock Richard, obtained a license from Queen Elizabeth to visit the exile in Antwerp with intent to persuade him to submit to the royal pleasure. Houghton was anxious to return but could not make terms with the court to retain his religion: he therefore remained in exile until his death, which occurred at Liege, June 2, 1580, aged 63. He had been of great assistance to Dr Allen in founding Douay College and on July 5, 1590, his body was carried from Liege to Douay . . .

His son and namesake, Thomas Houghton, went with his father into exile, and was not recognised on the escheat in 1580. He was placed with Dr Allen at Douay College, whence he left to visit his father in Brabant in 1577. He probably returned, for he matriculated in the University of Douay, was ordained priest and proceeded to the English Mission. He had no sooner arrived in Lancashire than he was seized and thrown into Salford gaol, where great numbers of recusants were confined. There his name appears in the lists of priests returned to the council by Edmund Trafford and Robert Worsley on April 13, 1582. Then his name is lost sight of.

There is a curiously laudatory reference to this Roman Catholic foundation of Douay at Reims in one of Shakespeare's early plays:

> 'I freely give unto you this young scholar that hath been long studying at Reims; as cunning in Greek and Latin and other tongues as his comrade in music and mathematics . . .'
> (TAMING OF THE SHREW, 2.1)

The allusion is pointed out in Clara Longworth de Chambrun's *Shakespeare Rediscovered* (Scribner's, 1938). She goes on to draw attention to another quotation suggesting that the playwright was familiar with the English version of the New Testament that was printed at Reims in 1583, and liberally dispersed through England by the missionaries:

> A small circumstance, but one of singular interest, indicates that when William Shakespeare made use of the parable of the Sowers from the Gospel of St. Matthew, he had the Reims translation in mind and not either the so-called 'Breeches' or 'Bishops' Bible. Though verbal, the evidence is striking. Down to the present day all Protestant Bibles employ the word *tares* in speak-

ing of the ill weeds sown among the wheat, whereas the Catholic texts use *cockle*.

Now, in the whole course of Shakespeare's work the word *tares* is never found, but when he recalls the parable of the sowers the word *cockle* appears in its place, as in the Reims translation:

> 'The Kingdom of heaven is resembled to a man who sowed good seeds in his field, but when men were asleepe his enemy came and oversowed cockle among the wheate, and went his way. And when the blade was shot up and had brought forth fruits, then appeared also the cockle . . . and the servants of the goodman of the house coming said to him, Sir didst thou not sow good seede in thy field, whence then hath it cockle?'

In *Love's Labour's Lost* we find:

> 'Sowed cockle reaps no corn'

and again in *Coriolanus* the same term appears in similar connexion:

> 'That cockle of Rebellion, Insolence, Sedition,
> Which we ourselves have ploughed for, sowed and scattered.'

Of course, there has long been debate about the theory that Shakespeare was a member of the Roman Catholic Church, and maintained that religion; ever since the Rev. Richard Davies, rector of Sapperton, Gloucestershire, in 1695, recorded in a memorandum on Shakespeare that 'He dyed a papist'. Many passages in the plays have been cited to show that the poet always avoided such a display of anti-Catholic prejudice as might have been expected to find high favour with his audience; and it has been maintained that, like A., he lacked courage to defend the Old Religion, yet could not find it in his heart to attack it.

To prove Shakespeare's familiarity with Roman Catholic phraseology, writers have cited Don John's pun: 'If I can cross him anyway, I bless myself every way.' Catholics still describe as 'blessing oneself' the action that Protestants call 'crossing oneself'.

Various speeches in the plays have also been said to indicate that the author was familiar with Catholic moral theology. In *All's Well that Ends Well*, Helena's:

> Why then, tonight
> Let us assay our plot: which if it speed
> Is wicked meaning in a lawful deed,
> And lawful meaning in a lawful act,
> Where both not sin, and yet a sinful fact
>
> (3.7.44)

is supposed to be informed by the Catholic philosophy of substitution and formal and material sin. A similar case is made from Posthumus's speech in gaol:

> My conscience, thou art fettered
> More than my shanks and wrists: you good gods give me
> The pertinent instrument to pick that bolt,
> Then, free for ever! Is't enough I am sorry?
> So children temporal fathers do appease;
> Gods are more full of mercy. Must I repent?
> I cannot do it better than in gyves,
> Desired more than constrained: to satisfy,

PLATE VII

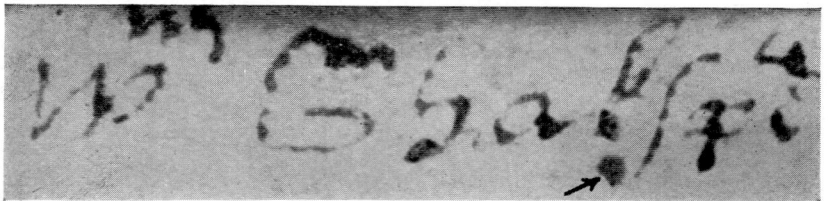

1. A signature of William Shakespeare, *1613*. Note abrupt termination of the long 's'.

2. 'Rebells' from H.v.f.xii. 3. 'Infidells' from H.iv.f.xxxii.

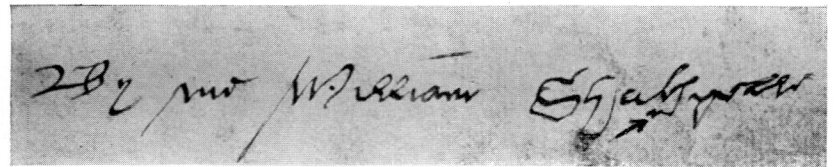

4. Signature on p. 3 of *1616* will. Again note the jerky tail of the long 's'.

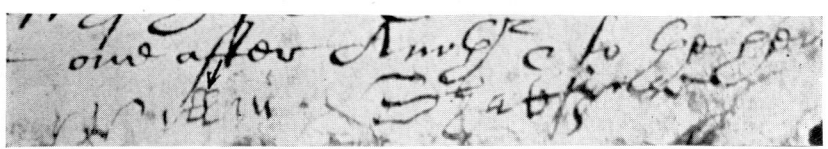

5. Signature on p. 2 of *1616* will. Note overlapping of 'll'.

COMPARISON OF HANDWRITING
(*See Appendix iii*)

PLATE VIII

6. *Contraction from 1612 signature. Note the angular loop of the 'l' (cf. 5).*

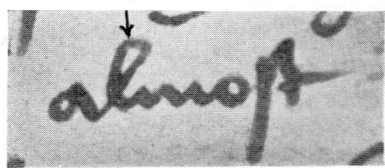

7. *'Almost' from H.iv.f.xxvii (cf. 5, 6).*

8. *'Smalle' from H.iv.f.i. (This overlapping 'll' is also found in the signature, not shown, of 10 March, 1613.)*

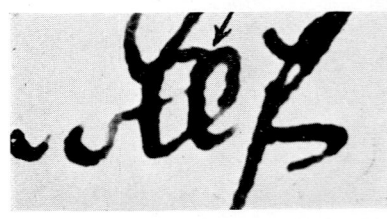

9. *'Wollf' from H.iv.f.xx. (cf. 5).*

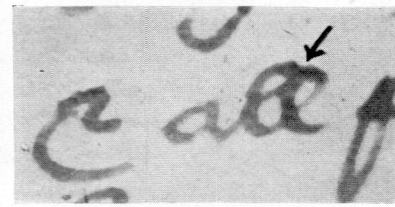

10. *Cf. 5.*

COMPARISON OF HANDWRITING (*cont.*)
(*See Appendix iii*)

THE ANNOTATOR

> If of my freedom 'tis the main part, take
> No stricter render of me than my all.
> (CYMBELINE, 5.4)

Here Posthumus is said to be thinking in Catholic terms, echoing the early divines who divided the Sacrament of Penance into the different parts of attrition, contrition, confession and satisfaction.

There is in *King Lear* an allusion to the misfortunes of a Stratford recusant which has not been much noted, though it was pointed out by Theobald. In *King Lear* (4.1) Edgar, pretending to his blind father that he is a madman, tells of the fiends:

> Obidicut; Hobbididance, prince of dumbness; Mahu, of stealing; Modo, of murder; Flibbertigibbet, of mopping and mowing, who since possesses chambermaids and waiting-women.

The devilish names in this passage seem to have come from Samuel Harsnett's *Declaration of Egregious Popish Impostures*, 1603. In this compilation of cases against English priests, Harsnett tells of one case where a priest named Robert Dibdale held a Mass in a house near Uxbridge, to exorcise devils alleged to be in possession of a chambermaid, one Sara Williams. The poor girl was forced to drink a 'holy potion' composed of a 'pint of sacke and sallet oyle . . . mingled with some kind of spices', after which she was quite naturally sick. Satanic voices were heard, 'and if you will not beleeve these, beleeve the devill himselfe in his Dialogue with Dibdale, crying in his devils roaring voyce that he came thither for money, money'. And 'Ma. Dibdale' is then recounted to have thrown out from the serving wench demons called *Frateretto, Fliberdigibett, Hoberdidance, Modoz,* and *Mohu.*

Shakespeare may have had some particular interest in reading this passage in Harsnett, for Robert Dibdale (or Debdale) was about the same age as Shakespeare, and the son of a Catholic farmer at Shottery; a neighbour to Anne Hathaway, and to the Richardsons and the Sandells—it will be recalled that Fulke Sandells and John Richardson were sureties to the marriage bond of William Shakespeare and Anne Hathaway on 28 November 1582.

Dibdale appears to have been a schoolfellow of Shakespeare's at the Grammar School, but later he was at Douay and Reims; it seems possible that he was taken thither by Simon Hunt in 1575. When Thomas Cottam, younger brother of John Cottam, schoolmaster at Stratford in 1579-82, returned to England from Reims in June 1580, he brought with him a letter from Dibdale and religious tokens for the folk at Shottery. Cottam was arrested and thrown into the Tower, and Dibdale's letter was confiscated – and thus preserved. Dibdale followed Cottam a week or two later and was also arrested.

Dibdale languished in the Gatehouse at Westminster until 20 September 1582, when he was released and, as Edgar I. Fripp in *Shakespeare Man and Artist* (O.U.P., 1938) observes, 'then may have been at home for a merry meeting about the time of Shakespeare's marriage with Anne Hathaway'. His imprisonment does not seem to have broken Dibdale's faith or his nerve; four years later he was again arrested, and after trial as a seminary priest and practiser of magic, was executed in December 1586.

If Shakespeare was one of the minority of Roman Catholic pupils at Stratford, perhaps he, like Robert Dibdale, stood by his master Simon Hunt, and eventually accompanied him to Douay? Dibdale apparently went to Rome with Hunt, and returned to Douay in December 1579, to train for the English Mission. If Shakespeare went with them it would have given him early in his life that first-hand acquaintance with Italy that so many writers have thought him to have possessed. It is a long shot, but not an illogical one.

And then from Italy or Douay, to Lea Hall in Lancashire? Well, we have seen that Richard Houghton in 1576 obtained a licence to visit his exiled half-brother Thomas Houghton at Antwerp. He was given a permit to stay abroad for two months, to take twenty pounds' foreign currency allowance, and to be attended by one servant. It may be that in the circle of English papists on the Continent he found a twelve-year-old boy who was inclined to fancy his future as a player more than as a priest, and was chafing to get back to England. Then Houghton may have left a Romanist servant with his half-brother at Antwerp, and in his stead taken back with him to Lancashire that boy, who later entered service at Lea Hall, and, to avoid reawakening the odium incurred by his departure from Stratford to Douay a year earlier under the wing of a papist pedagogue, called himself Shakeshafte instead of Shakespeare.

THE ANNOTATOR

Perhaps this kite is flying very high; but it sails trimly enough.

There is little doubt that in his childhood Shakespeare would have known enthusiastic Roman Catholics in the family circle. His father's sister Domina was a nun at Wroxhall, and when the convent was dissolved she retired to Stratford and died there when her nephew was fourteen.

His mother's family of Arden were well-known Catholics, and connected with the Catesbys. In 1583 Mary Arden's cousin Edward Arden, of Park Hall, was indicted for treason. He and his son-in-law were executed, and his family imprisoned. And we have seen above, the reasons for supposing that John Shakespeare was a Catholic.[1]

More urgently than before, the question presents itself, and even now must go unanswered for lack of cast-iron direct evidence – did William Shakespeare peruse and annotate this copy of Halle?

One question *can* be answered: how does this neat and fluent writing in the margins compare with the accepted signatures of William Shakespeare?

Palaeographers have not so far established with certainty the nature of Shakespeare's handwriting: bare and sometimes contracted signatures are a poor basis on which to identify continuous script.

[1] The question of John Shakespeare's religion is dealt with by Fripp, *op. cit.* 156: 'He was, beyond doubt, an obstinate recusant', and by Chambers, vi, 380, where he examines the question of John Shakespeare's supposed 'spiritual will', much canvassed by Catholic writers

THE ANNOTATOR

As H. T. F. Rhodes points out in Appendix iii, the poet was a curiously erratic signatory (which increases the difficulty of comparison); but he clearly used the 'secretary' or provincial hand. In this type of hand is also written the MS. section of the play of *Sir Thomas More* which A. W. Pollard and others tried in 1923 to establish as being in Shakespeare's hand. Acceptance here cannot be absolute; the hand of a reviser or a scribe could easily have been responsible for it. Moreover, though the palaeographers have pointed out the similarity between the 'ascenders' and 'descenders' in the hand of the *More* 'addition', and those present in the last autograph of the poet, it may fairly be said that these same characteristics can be found in many examples of the professional secretary or cursive hand of the sixteen and seventeenth centuries.

The same is true of the 'spurred' 'a', which the writer of the *More* addition and Shakespeare both use. Professional copyists and scriveners used it too; and Shakespeare often did not, but wrote an unspurred 'a'. The annotator of our copy of Halle's *Chronicle* wrote in this cursive style without the spurred 'a'.

All that can be said is that identification of Shakespeare with A. can be neither proved nor disproved by comparing the annotations with the signatures or the *More* 'addition'. It must be remembered that the annotations in Halle would have been made at least twenty years earlier than the signatures.

The detailed technical examination of the problem follows in Appendix iii. Meanwhile, it is interesting to observe two pen-habits of our annotator. When he writes a word ending in 'n' or 'm', he brings the last stroke down and curls it under. His 'S' is unusual, swift and economically formed.

Now these characteristics are identical with certain personal features of the hand of a man whose handwriting appears in the Stratford-on-Avon Council Book of 1564, the year of Shakespeare's birth. By that date they were already unusual; they are common features of fifteenth century hands, but in the sixteenth century only appear in provincial documents or old-fashioned 'copy-book' writings. Shakespeare seems to have been an old-fashioned speller; perhaps his hand was old-fashioned, too? Indeed, it is probable that it was; for at Stratford Grammar School, spelling and penmanship both came under the direction of an old-fashioned pedagogue, Walter Roche, a 'provincial' from Lancashire.

In our plan of the young Shakespeare's progress, and our guesses about the track of the *Chronicle*, we have not hitherto attempted to plot any hypothetical intersection: we have not found enough evidence to feel able to hazard a definite time and place for the playwright's perusal and annotation of the book. He may have found it at Lea and carried it to Rufford, perhaps after working on it during his year at Stratford. Or others may have brought it to Rufford or to Knowsley, and Shakespeare may have studied it in a library of one of those great houses.

If our identification of Robert Worsley is correct, and our conjecture about his possession of the book, it must have been years later that it found its way back to its rightful owners, and thence along the line to the Worsleys.

Some clue to date, and thence to place, may perhaps be found in the stopping-place of the marginal notes. A.'s last entries refer to the very beginning of Henry VI's reign:

> *duke of exeter governour*
> *duke of bedford regen(t)*
> *duke of glocester protect(or)* . . .
> *The dolphin proclam(ed) himsellf Kinge of fra(nce)*
> *by the name of Charles the VIIth*

and there he gives up his work on the book.

Dover Wilson believes that *Henry VI Part I*, as acted by Strange's Men at the Rose, was a 'rush job' put together by various hands, the second and third parts of the trilogy being already in existence. 'The haste with which, as I believe, the whole thing was knocked together suggests the calling in of all available writers for the composition of the verse, once the play had been plotted from the chronicles.'

If the play originally went on to the stocks at Knowsley, and Shakespeare was known there to be a student of the York and Lancaster history, he would naturally have been one of the writers pulled in. The framework and plotting of the play had been dealt with by Nashe and Greene, he was only required to contribute colour and life; for which no close study of the chronicles was necessary. So if about that time he reached the reign of Henry VI in his own reading, he might have decided there to break off his close study of the *Chronicle*.

Alternatively, if, all along, he had perused the *Chronicle* with the ultimate creation of a dramatic cycle in mind, and if during the course of his work he heard that a Henry VI play was already planned or in preparation elsewhere, he may have decided not to cover the same ground with his own researches but to confine his creative attention to the earlier reigns.

Perhaps it is sanguine to look for significance in A.'s stopping-place; and if *Henry VI Part I* was in fact not composed until 1591-2, and then in London, the surmises above are clearly at war with other of our ideas. Perhaps the scope of the notes is just another of those tempting coincidences that we have encountered at every turn. For A.'s neglect of Henry VI's reign, after his close study of the previous kings, certainly seems to find a reflection in the pattern of Shakespeare's work on the contention of the Houses of York and Lancaster.

XI

*Keep house and ply his book, welcome his friends,
Visit his countrymen . . .*
             (TAMING OF THE SHREW I.I.201)

WE have shewn above the importance that we have attached to family relationships as a help to the discovery of the track of the annotated *Chronicle*, as well as of the young Shakespeare. The Newport-Houghton-Hesketh connexion led us to look more closely into the activities of players in Lancashire. The Houghton-Worsley kinship gave us a clue to the movements of the book. The Holcrofts, Fittons, Levesons, Stanleys, have been mentioned as something more than chance acquaintances.

All these connexions and relationships can only be clearly followed with the help of genealogical charts. Through such charts we can also trace certain important and influential family connexions of William Shakespeare, which seem in the past to have attracted less attention than they deserve.

In making up these charts my ally has been Norman Long-Brown, an old friend, who once confronted with the problem lived for weeks the life of a hermit in the British Museum and Somerset House. His occasional enthusiastic reappearances at Clifford's Inn, and his confident determination that no family, however ancient or obscure, is untraceable, provided invaluable support in the long search which has filled most of the waking hours of a decade of my life.

Eventually Norman began to turn up with scraps of paper upon which he had crammed (often confusedly, so great was his excitement) such written material, culled from printed and manuscript records, as to suggest that at last the truth of Shakespeare's youth, spent among 'divers of worship', was breaking through the mists and cobwebs of three centuries. And when, a year or two later, Norman arrived at Hampstead to deliver his finished job, the floor of the sitting room was covered with sheets of foolscap to which pieces of writing paper were pinned. From the accumulated work of long months spent among musty records, wills and county visitations, we could now see a pattern emerging, of the poet's relatives, patrons, fellows, business associates and trustees; from boyhood to maturity.

To plot the pattern was the next task which fell to my wife, and she planned a series of interrelated charts from Norman's tabular notes. These were to occupy all her leisure for weeks to come until at last we could examine the pattern before us – a tapestry of the midland and northern counties of Elizabethan England; a tapestry of noble houses, manors and theatres, peopled with Shakespeare's familiars.

When Robin Greene, dying miserably, railed against the *'upstart Crow; a Tygers hart wrapt in a Players hyde'*; and 'being an absolute *Iohannes fac totum*, is in his own conceit the only Shake-scene in a country', the printer of the pamphlet Henry Chettle, himself a writer and dramatist, sprang to an apology. His author was dead, and so Chettle penned and published *Kind-Harts Dreame, conteining fiue Apparitions with their Inuectiues against abuses raigning*, 1592, in which he offered regret for the part he had played in editing Greene's *Groatsworth of wit* with its attack:

> I am as sory as if the originall fault had been my fault, because myselfe haue seene his [*Shakespeare's*] demeanour no less ciuill than he excelent in the qualitie he professes: Besides, diuers of worship haue reported his vprightnes of dealing, which argues his honesty, and his facetious grace in writing, that aprooues his Art.

Divers of worship! This brought to mind the scores of commentators, who for a century and more have argued Shakespeare's gentle birth and high social position. For instance, William Henty, writing in a little book 'for private circulation', *Shakespeare. With some Notes on his Early Biography*, London, 1882:

> Whilst so much attention of late has been directed to detect indications of real characters in Shakespeare's works, especially all allusions to his own personal experiences, and, among others, of references to his own son, I believe there is a much larger field than has yet been traced for such discoveries. It seems strange how those I am about to indicate have been overlooked, so plain as they appear, and of such direct bearing and importance in the elucidation of Shakespeare's early career, and so of his whole life and character.
> Dyce, who ought to have been the guardian of his fame, gives a contemptuous summary of

his career, speaks in discourteous terms of his wife, and shows no love for his family. Had he looked back in the Heralds' Office, he would have found undoubted testimonials of a family of worship in the stock from which Shakespeare sprung.

Soon after the annotated *Chronicle* had pointed a line to genealogical research through the autograph of its first owner, Sir Richard Newport of High Ercall, many tributaries were found joining the main stream which, flowing from Shropshire, joined with another from Warwickshire and made its way into Cheshire and Lancashire.

Following the course of the stream, there seemed to be 'families of worship' on every side, directly or indirectly connected with Shakespeare. Here indeed was a job, and no easy one either, to confirm and qualify these *divers of worship* and so fill the sadly-missing gaps in the poet's biography.

When Shakespeare in the second part of *Henry VI* speaks of:

> The rampant bear chain'd to the ragged staff

he refers to the ancient device of the Arden family. Shakespeare claimed descent from the house of Arden and the right to bear its arms. In this he was supported by the Heralds, who described his grandfather, Robert Arden, as a 'gentleman of worship'. The Ardens of Wilmcote, a village three miles north-west of Stratford, were a minor branch of the Ardens of Park Hall, between Birmingham and Coleshill, one of whom was Sheriff of Warwickshire in 1438, another High Sheriff in 1575.

Mary, the poet's mother, in marrying John

Shakespeare, did not marry beneath her, for in the document of 1599, when her famous son applied for the grant of arms, it is affirmed upon 'credible reports' of 'John Shakespeare, now of Stratford-upon-Avon, in the county of Warwick, gentleman,' 'that his parent, great-grandfather, and late antecessor, for his faithful and approved service to the late most prudent prince King Henry VII of famous memory, was advanced and rewarded with lands and tenements, given to him in those parts of Warwickshire, where they have continued by some descents in good reputation and credit'. Knight observes, 'On the 22nd of August 1485, there was a battle fought for the crown of England, a short battle ending in a decisive victory. The battle-field was Bosworth', and asks, 'Was there in that victorious army of the Earl of Richmond – which Richard denounced as a "company of traitors, thieves, outlaws and runagates" – an Englishman bearing the name of Chacksper, or Shakespeyre, or Schakespere, or Schakespeire, or Shakespeare – a martial name, however spelt?' Of the warlike achievements of John Shakespeare's great-grandfather there is no record, but then his name or his deeds would have no interest for us unless there had been born, eighty years after Bosworth Field, a direct descendant from him

> Whose muse, full of high thought's invention,
> Doth like himself heroically sound.

The stream and tributaries of these families of Arden and Shakespeare, are for us and our narrative of discovery, exciting. From the great Salopian houses of Corbet, Newport and Leveson we get our first sight of Shakespeare's 'divers of worship', which on the first chart in Appendix i tell their own story.

On this chart we begin to move with the poet among his kindred. From the line of Sir Robert Corbet of Moreton Corbet and his wife Elizabeth Vernon of Haddon, together with the descent of his sister Mary Corbet, who married Thomas Lacon of Willey, there follows a remarkable progression. The union of Mary Lacon, firstly with Thomas Acton of Sutton, produced Joyce Acton, daughter and heiress, who married Sir Thomas Lucy of Charlecote, the supposed persecutor of the poet; and secondly with George Vernon, a son – Sir John Vernon of Hodnet, Shropshire. Sir John's marriage with Elizabeth Devereux gave to the Virgin Queen a Maid of Honour in their daughter Elizabeth Vernon, and to Henry Wriothesley, Earl of Southampton, a bride.

A near cousin to Elizabeth Vernon was Southampton's friend and the Queen's favourite, Robert, Earl of Essex; a more distant cousin William Shakespeare. It is not difficult to surmise how the poet met his first patron, indeed if we look further we may ask just what part Shakespeare played behind the performance of *Richard II* by the Globe Company on the eve of the ill-fated Essex conspiracy, in which Southampton was implicated and later disgraced? Both these morning-stars of the Elizabethan firmament were kindred with the young and successful poet-playwright.

THE ANNOTATOR

Sir Robert Corbet's daughter Anne, by her marriage with Thomas Newport of High Ercall, brought into the world Sir Richard Newport, later to be Lord of Ercall, and to be the owner of a particular copy of Halle's *Chronicle* which may have been read, and annotated, by William Shakeshafte; which may have had its stirring prose transmuted into the *Histories* of William Shakespeare. Sir Richard's daughter Magdalen, who married Richard Herbert of Montgomery, was friend and patron of John Donne and bore her husband three distinguished sons: Edward, Lord Herbert of Cherbury; George Herbert, parson and poet, the 'sweet singer of the Temple'; and Sir Henry Herbert, Master of the Revels. Of Sir Richard's other children, his son Sir Francis Newport, Sheriff of Shropshire, married Beatrix Lacon; and their son Sir Richard Newport wed Rachel daughter of Sir John Leveson, brother of Shakespeare's trustee and friend, William Leveson.

The chart shows other interesting conjunctions. To the right, Elizabeth Corbet gives her hand to Robert Arden of Park Hall, Warwickshire; her sister Anna to Edward Mitton (whose mother was the daughter of Sir Edward Greville), a name familiar to Shakespearian detectives. Anna and Edward's son Richard Mitton is mentioned in the famous letter from Richard Quiney to William Shakespeare:

> Loving Countryman I am bold of you as a friend, craving your help with thirty Pounds upon Mr Bushell's and my security, or Mr

Mitton's with me . . . (from the Bell in Carter Lane the 25 October 1598).

Chart Two brings us to the great northern families of Fitton, Holcroft and Hesketh. From the line of Sir Edward Fitton, of Gawsworth, Cheshire, who was gathered to his fathers in 1547/8, alliance was made with the Shropshire Levesons by the marriage of his daughter Mary, born in 1529, with Sir Richard Leveson of Lilleshall. Their descent is interesting, as we find his son Sir Richard wedding Anne Corbet, daughter of Sir Andrew of Moreton Corbet. Their son the third Sir Richard (1569-1605) sea-dog and Admiral of the Fleet, who married Lady Margaret Howard daughter of the Earl of Nottingham, High Admiral of England, enjoyed a liaison with his Cheshire cousin Mary Fitton, the second of the Queen's Northern Maids of Honour, who had also bestowed her favours upon the Earl of Pembroke, one of Shakespeare's 'incomparable brethren'. Admiral Leveson's executors of his will were his cousins, Sir Edward Fitton, Sir Robert Harley and Sir John Leveson, brother of William Leveson, Shakespeare's friend and co-trustee, with Thomas Savage of Rufford, in the Globe Theatre.

Francis, brother of the first Mary Fitton (who married the first Sir Richard Leveson), took as wife Katherine Nevill, widow of the eighth Earl of Northumberland. Her son, Sir Charles Percy of Dumbleton, Gloucester, had a lively interest in the plays of Shakespeare; indeed a letter of his in the *State Papers, Domestic* quotes 'Justice Silence or

THE ANNOTATOR

Justice Shallow'. It was he who persuaded the players of Shakespeare's Company at the Globe to revive the 'old' play of the deposition of *Richard II*; and after dining at Gunter's, the day before the Essex rising, in company with Lord Monteagle, Sir Christopher Blount, Sir Charles Percy, Edward Bushell and others, he crossed the Thames to the Globe to witness this most treasonable performance. That the players had been given forty shillings more than their usual payment was suspicious enough, and had Sir Charles Percy stuck to his plays for their own sake, leaving treason to theatrical counterfeit, he would have kept his head on his shoulders. Being with Southampton, Shakespeare's patron and friend, a supporter of the ill-starred Essex, Percy was executed, and the Globe actors severely censured for their afternoon's work.

In passing we may mark the name above of Edward Bushell, brother of Thomas Bushell, surety with Richard Mitton, offered to Shakespeare by Quiney in his letter of 1598. Bushell – Sir Edward – was in the service of Ferdinando, Lord Strange, and as a gentleman retainer very likely wore the Stanley badge of the Eagle and Child on his sleeve.

The Fitton tree throws its branches into Lancashire. The third Sir Edward Fitton took the hand of Alice Holcroft, daughter of Sir John Holcroft of Lancaster, by whom he had three children, Sir Edward Fitton (the fourth), 1572-1619, Anne Fitton and Mary Fitton, the 'Dark Lady'. Alice Holcroft's aunt and namesake married Sir Thomas Hesketh of Rufford, Lancashire, to whom William Shakeshafte was commended by Alexander Houghton of Lea Hall. Her niece Isobel, daughter of her brother Sir Thomas Holcroft, wed the third Earl of Rutland, whose nephew the fifth Earl of Rutland was a friend and fellow member of Gray's Inn with Shakespeare's Earl of Southampton.

In *Chart Three* we find another Leveson – Elizabeth – the daughter of Mary Fitton (whom we have noticed on Chart Two) marrying William Sheldon, the son of the founder of the far-famed tapestry looms in Worcestershire and Warwickshire. His brother Ralph Sheldon married Anne Throckmorton, sister-in-law to Edward Arden, who was kindred with Shakespeare's mother Mary Arden. The children of this union must have had more than one memory of the poet since Elizabeth Sheldon married Sir John Russell the half-brother of Thomas Russell, Esquire (1570-1634), overseer of the will of Shakespeare; and Elizabeth's nephew William (son of her brother Edward), cherished his copy of Shakespeare's *Comedies Histories and Tragedies*, 1623, preserving it, as did his descendants, so well that in our times this identical copy of the First Folio is still immaculate and splendid in its original binding. Known as the Burdett-Coutts copy it now rests, the pride of the Folger Shakespeare Library, at Washington D.C.

The Sheldons bring other Shakespearian links: particularly Anne, the sister of the brothers William and Ralph by her two marriages; firstly to Francis Savage, and secondly to Antony Daston. Her daughter Anne Daston's husband, Ralph Huband,

THE ANNOTATOR

not only had dealings with the poet in 1605 with the sale of tithes, but was the cousin of Thomas Nash, whose sons Anthony and John were legatees of Shakespeare. But it is Anne's first marriage with Francis Savage that stirs my imagination more vividly.

Anne and Francis Savage had four children, Mary, William, Antony and Walter. Mary wed Thomas Combe of Stratford-upon-Avon, to whom Shakespeare left his sword. Antony's son John sold land to Henry Condell, one of Shakespeare's fellows and joint-editor with Heminges of the posthumous First Folio in 1623. The marriage in 1581 of Walter Savage to Elizabeth Hall (daughter of Richard Hall and Joyce Blount) brings in that line of Savage which presents itself on Chart Three. Here are shown the parties to certain transactions with Henry Condell and the Washbourne family in 1617-19, and their Shakespearian connexions; but more importantly, the line of Savage which joins the discoveries of Mr Barnard[1] to our own search for Shakespeare's 'hidden' years.

Look at *Chart Three*, and from the union of Walter and Elizabeth Savage follow the arrows down to where Walter Savage the fifth links with the name of Cecilia Oldys.

Mr Barnard states: 'The Hanley Court Collection was originally made through the medium of Cecilia Oldys, by her marriage with Walter Savage of

---

[1] E. A. B. Barnard, F.S.A., in *New Links with Shakespeare* (Cambridge, 1930) describes his discovery of documents now known as the Hanley Court Collection and deposited on permanent loan by the owner, Sir Offley Wakeman, at Birmingham Reference Library

Broadway, who died before the 21st September 1721 – and afterwards by her marriage with John Newport of Hanley Court. She was born in 1694, her father being the Rev. Thomas Oldys, of Tingewick near Buckingham, who for many years possessed the rectory of Quinton, Co. Gloucester, lying off the main road between Broadway and Stratford-upon-Avon. As Cecilia Newport, she is still commemorated in the old church of St. Eadburgha at Broadway ... her death is recorded as having taken place on 21st March 1766, when she was aged seventy-two. John Newport died in 1760 aged sixty. The above named Thomas Oldys was related to William Oldys (1696-1761), the antiquary of whom the curiously interesting statement is made that he "had engaged to furnish a bookseller in the Strand, whose name was Walker, with ten years of the life of Shakespeare unknown to the biographers and commentators, but he died and made no sign of the projected work".'

As Cecilia's first husband, Walter Savage, was a descendant of Savage of Rock Savage, a northern family allied to the Stanleys; a branch of which included Thomas Savage of Rufford, who was Shakespeare's friend; it seems possible that some account of the youth and beginnings of Shakespeare in Lancashire and Shropshire was given orally by Walter Savage to William Oldys. Cecilia, her husband, and the antiquary were exact contemporaries, so time is in agreement with such a possibility.

On this note of expectation we turn to *Chart Four*.

Alexander Houghton of Lea's grandfather, who died at the turn of the sixteenth century, was kindred with John Houghton of Pendleton, Lancashire, who by his marriage with Grace Nowell, daughter of Roger Nowell of Read and his wife Margaret Hesketh (his second wife was Grace Towneley) became allied to the great houses of Nowell and Towneley. Sir Richard Houghton, by his first marriage to Alice Asheton, had two sons: Thomas Houghton (who helped to found Douay), and Alexander Houghton of Lea. Alexander took as wife Elizabeth, daughter of Gabriel Hesketh of Aughton. Alexander's father married again, this time with Alice Morley; their son Thomas Houghton was killed in the brawl at Lea Hall on 21 November 1589.

This latter Thomas was Auditor to the Earl of Derby, and by his wife Anne Kighley had three sons. One, Sir Richard Houghton, married Katherine Gerard, daughter of Sir Gilbert Gerard of Staffordshire. (Sir Gilbert, Attorney-General and Master of the Rolls, was a cousin of the Fittons, his mother being Margaret Holcroft.) The ill-fated Thomas Houghton's namesake and third son became directly connected with the Houghtons of Pendleton and the Nowells of Read, by his marriage to Catherine Houghton, and thereby brings us to another Alexander Houghton, whose wife Maud Aspinall was a kinswoman of Alexander Aspinall, the schoolmaster of Stratford and friend of William Shakespeare; for whom the poet made a 'posy' to accompany the gift of a pair of gloves when Alexander from Lancashire went courting Ann

Shaw, mother of Shakespeare's friend Julius Shaw: The Gift is small, the Will is all Alexander Aspinall.

This is something more than a good story. In Appendix vi to this book we shall show that the Stratford schoolmaster was a Towneley connexion and a Hesketh one too. It was Robert Nowell of Read Hall who assisted the young Alexander Aspinall to Brasenose, Oxford, as a 'poor scholar' and was a benefactor of Edmund Spenser also.

Chart Five covers familiar ground, for Shakespeare and his Warwickshire contemporaries have been well catalogued by the pen of Charlotte Carmichael Stopes; but certain links from the preceding charts bring us to William Shakespeare of Stratford-upon-Avon, Gentleman, and his family and descendants. Throckmortons, Sheldons, Grevilles, Russells and Quineys . . . the Winters, Catesby and Tresham – the Gunpowder Plotters . . . take their places on the Chart and above them all the line of Willoughby, leading to Henry Willoughby, author of the poem *Willobie his Avisa, or the true picture of a Modest Maid and of a chast and constant wife*, 1594, of which Professor Hotson has written in *I, William Shakespeare* (1937). Henry Willoughby's son, William Willoughby, as Hotson shows, married Eleanor Bampfield, daughter of Hugh Bampfield, in 1590, thus forging an important link between Willoughby and Shakespeare; for Eleanor's sister Katherine Bampfield married Thomas Russell, Shakespeare's friend and overseer to his will. After the death of his wife Katherine, Thomas Russell later married in 1603, Anne Digges, mother of Leonard Digges who joined Ben Jonson, Hugh Holland and James Mabbe in the prefatory eulogy to the First Folio in 1623:

> *Shake-speare, at length they pious fellowes give*
> *The world they Workes, by which, out-live*
> *Thy Tombe, thy name must when that stone is rent*
> *And Time dissolves they Stratford Moniment . . .*

We have come full cycle in our inquiry of Shakespeare's 'divers of worship', and in the process surely marked the 'map of all his days'. It takes a great scroll to carry the names of those families and individuals either directly or indirectly connected with the poet in his all-too-brief life. Yet it is not difficult to see a pattern from which one might begin to plot a new biography for him.

In making a new *Life*, any writer must take old threads and bring to them the bright new skeins, spun by the industry of contemporary scholars on both sides of the Atlantic, to make the tapestry complete – or nearly so. For the tale is by no means told. The compass of the present book can only take in pointers to the material for further explorations.

For my part, I can never forget the debt we owe to the early nineteenth-century bibliophile for preserving an imperfect, if interesting, book; to fortuitous circumstance, which brought it to the Gate House – a refuge perhaps from wartime 'salvage' paper-drives: but most of all to the original owner

THE ANNOTATOR

of this *Chronicle* of Edward Halle, the Lord of Ercall, who so long ago on a spring day took his quill, and in the margins of his new possession left for us the cipher to the secret of Shakespeare's 'hidden' years,
'Rychard Newport'
and

APPENDICES

i

Genealogical Tables

(see folding charts at the end of the book)

ii

Transcription of the Annotations

HENRY IV

f. i	by concorde smalle thinges doithe growe by discorde gret thin(ges) dothe awaye flowe
f. ii	... on of a ... of the howses ... caster
f. iii	the duke of herford entryd the lystes The Kynge prese(nt) with many armyd
f. iv[a]	The justynge was (st)opped sodenly by (t)he Kynge (He)nry duke of herford (ba)nisshed for X year (Th)omas duke of Norfo(lk) banisshid for ever (the) duke of norfolk (dy)ed at venice (for) thought shortly
f. iv[b]	the peple lamentyd the duke of herfo(rd) who was honorab(ly) entertayned in fr(ance) John of gaunt (died) The Kinge ceazed and kepte the dukedom of Lancastre from he(nry) the right heyre

THE ANNOTATOR

	Edmunde duke (of) yorke dyd sto(mack) the matter and a(fter) the murther of (his) brother Thomas (of) woodstocke duk(e) (of) glocester
	lacke of assur(ed) and frendly com(panions)
f. v^a	(t)he embassie of (T)homas Arundell archebishop of cant' (to) henry duke of (la)ncaster and herford
f. vi^a	The duke arryved (in) england at raven (sp)urre
f. vi^b	Kynge Richard ca(me) owt of Ireland b(ut) at his comynge w(as) discommfetid
	Kinge Ric' helde the c(astle) of flint
f. vii^a	(K)ynge Richard (t)aken and sent to the (To)wer at london
	(A)rticles declaryd (in) parliament against (K)inge Richard
f. ix^a	Kinge Richarde consentid to be deposyd
	A solempne resignation of the crowne by Kinge Richard
	nota for flaterye and wanton and voluptuose pleasure
f. ix^b	A gr
	A gret some of money delivered 300000 li
f. x^a	Dyvisyon ones entred never ended tyll the heares males of bothe (t)he howses yorke and lancastre were destroyed
	A sleight counsell
f. x^b	Kinge henry chalenge(d) the crowne by conqu(est) and by adoption

APPENDIX II

              The bisshop of carle(ile) spake to late but yet very stoutlye
              The bisshop attac(hed) for his sayinge
              A conclusyon against the Kinge Richarde

f. xi^a   Kinge henrye pardonid offenders and avaunced his frendes

f. xii^a   here he begynneth to rayle   [*erased*]
         counsel agenst henry the 1111th
         a justinge at oxford

f. xii^b   conspiracy by indenture and othe
         the names of sondr(y) pieces of armour

f. xiii^a   The openings of the conspiracye by chaunce

f. xiii^b   the treason detecyd
         Magdalen represent(s) King Richard
         ['*publyshed Idole*' *underlined*]

f. xiv^a   a campe at hownslow heath
         the baylif of ancester assaultyd the conspiratowes
         execution   execution
                        Edward

f. xiv^b   Magdalen beheadyd
         Richard Kynge dyed of famyn

f. xv^a   Kynge Richard fought manfullye befor deathe as some saye
         a soden repentance

f. xv^b   the frenche men dyd stomake the death of K(ing) Richard

f. xvii^a   Owen in wales a newe conspiratour
         an armye against owen

THE ANNOTATOR

f. xvii^b	busynes emonge the scottes
	warre against the scottes
	chirches and religiouse howses sparyd
f. xviii^a	20000 men of scottes
	(h)enry lord percey called henrye hotspore
f. xviii^b	many slayne
	Kynge henry his yorn(ey) into Wales
	Ayed of frenchmen against the Kynge
f. xix^a	yll fortune to the frenche souldiers
f. xix^b	A brute off fame th(at) Kynge Richard lyved althoughe he was se(en) dead
	the practize of Rebells in bylles and ballades upon postes and castes in stretes
f. xx^a	Kynge henry maryed to Jane duches of brytane at Winchester
	cometa
	The pearcyes offendyd for prysoners
	the pearcyes forsake the Kynge
	a prophecie of the Mollwarpe, the dragon the lyon the wollf
f. xxi^a	‡ (h)e inveahithe against prophe(c)ies of the wellshmen
f. xxi^b	an exhortation
	a copye of articl(es)
f. xxii^a	1 article the clayme of the crowne
	2 articles the taxes
	3 article the deathe of Kinge richard
	4 article the defeacting of E. Mortymer
f. xxii^b	5 article they complayne ageyinste Knightes of th(e) parliament electyd

APPENDIX II

                6 article for not raunso(ming) E. Mortymer etc.
                the Answer of Kynge henrye
                the crye of the battayle

f. xxiii[a]	A good corage of the prince a gret slaughter
f. xxiii[b]	owen glender dyed of honger A seage against the castell of marke by the frenchmen
f. xxiv[a]	Ayde owt of Calyse A numbre of frenchmen taken
f. xxiv[b]	A provocation to a combat of the Kinge by the duke of orlians An Answer ‡A Kinge ough(te) to answer no chalen(ge) but to his pere with a further grave answer
f. xxv[a]	vi M frenchmen assaulted iii C englisshe men and gatte no honour No frenchmen slayne lorde thomas the Kinges sonne revenged the iniuryes
f. xxv[b]	A syege intendyd against calice but no(t) endyd A newe conspiratie of the earle of northumberland and others
f. xxvi[a]	certayne apprehendyd and sufferyd he reprehendythe the reports of some writers an other execution An other execution

THE ANNOTATOR

f. xxvi^b　The prince of Wales with the duke of yorke spoylyd the borders of Scotland
the souldiers dyd mete clothe with ther bowes
Sr Robert Vinefrevile captayne callyd of the scottes Robyn Mendmarket
An other rumor of Kynge Richard yet to be alyve

f. xxvii^a　The Kynge fledde by sea from the plage and was almost taken with the frenchmen
The lorde Camoys quytt by his peares
lady philip maryed to the Kinge of denmarke
Robert Kinge of scotland aged made his brother the first duke of albany governor of scotland
A fetche of Wallter to distroye the Kinges sede

f. xxvii^b　Walter governer of scotland hongersterv(ed) his nephew David the prince and kylled a woman that gave (him) mylke of hir brest(es) with a rede
provision for the oth(er) sonne of scotland James

f. xxviii^a　The causes of mischeff

f. xxviii^b　note for the love of foren princes, that it defendythe from civile sedition
A wyttye and pith(ye) letter endyd
The prince of scotland brought to windsor
Robert Kynge of scot(tes) dyed for thought of his sonnis evell intertaigment

APPENDIX II

f. xxix^a James Kinge of scottland 18 yeares prisoner was excellent in lerninge in martiall feates that scottland was therby reducyd from barbarose savagenes.
A new rebellyon of the ... earle of northumberland and taken by the shriff of yorkshire and beheadid
A spoyle of a towne in brytayne

f. xxix^b A C.M. ducates paid to the earle of Kent at his mariage at S. Mary overeyse
A frost contynued XV wekes
The Kinge of frau(nce) frenetike
a grudge betwene the duke of burgoyne and the duke of orleans

f. xxx^a divisyon had almost decayed fraunce with utter ruyne
The duke of orleaunce shamefully slayne and the facte iustified by the duke of burgoyne and doctor petit a precher
An othe taken and not regardyd
forther discention betwene the dukes and ayde send owt of england

f. xxx^b The englisshe arche(rs) sent home befor the w(ar) fully endyd
Kinge henrye somewha(t) at rest from civile discenscyon creatyd his sonnis dukes at a parliament

f. xxxi^a John duke of burgoyne had charles the frenche Kynge in soche sobiection that he made him to be armed against his nephew the duke of orleaunce

THE ANNOTATOR

              offers made to Kinge henrye in articles for to ayde them against the duke of burgoyne
              The duchye of Guyen to englandes right
              Mariage offeryd
              landes and treasures offerid
              ayde promised
              they promised to recognise guyen to be englisshe
              homage promised
              deliveraunce of townes XX promised

f. xxxi[b]   two dukes and one earle shuld holde of the Kyng pountiew, angulesme perrigot and iiii castelles
              The Kynge henry promised ayde to the duke of orleaunce with his complices
              The earle of S. paule foyled agayne

f. xxxii[a]   A siege to bourges by the frenche Kynge against his nephew
              C   M
              viii horsemen ix archers of England sent by the (Kinge)
              A fayned peace spredde abrode
              The dolphin concluded a peace with the duke of orleaunce to be rydde of the englisshemen

f. xxxii[b]   The duke of orleaunce dispatchid the englisshe armye with some moneye payed and pledges for the rest
              The duke of orleaunce in highe favor with the fr(enche) Kynge

APPENDIX II

After he was enemye to england and was prisoner ther xxiiii yeare
A parliament called for to conclude warre against infidelles
That counsell toke not place

f. xxxiii^a Kinge henrye semithe to confesse that he had the crowne wrongefullye and died Ao dñi 1413. he raigned xiii yeares and v monethes. buryed at canterburye.

HENRY V

f. i^b 9th of aprile 1405 henr(y) the Vth beganne to re(ign)
honours brought to the Kynge good maner(s)
Kinge henrye beinge but prince strake th(e) chief justice on the fa(ce) for imprisoninge of a wanton companyon of his
All flatterers and olde companions banisshid x myle from the courte

f. ii^a Sage counsellers chosen
Suche prince suche people
Two Kinges for lacke of sober sadnes brogt to calamitye. Ric 2 Edward 2
[*with line*]

f. ii^b he beganne to reforme bothe the clergie and th(e) laytye
he promotyd learnid men
Kinge Richardes bodye translated
The author wrote ((if) he dyd wryte it) in the afternoone   [*erased*]

135

THE ANNOTATOR

f. iii^a   certen persones sent to the counsell at constance
note that when he speakethe of the pope he shewithe himself to be of the englisshe schisme a favorer   [erased]
John Wickliff, John husse and Jherome of prage Sr John oldcastell lord cobham condemnid for heresye

f. iii^b   lord Cobham brake owt of the towre
heretikes and traytors hanged and burned
‡
A parliament at leices(ter)

f. iv^a   nota that a byll was framyd against temporall landes of the spirituall men
‡
Allways lying [erased]
‡
‡

f. iv^b   The right tytle to Normande Aquytayne Angeo, Mayne, Gaxony and all fraunce to the Kinge apperteigninge
note the exposition

f. v^a   Thre partes of fraunce belgique Celtique and Aquitayne
Hugh Capet an usurper of the crowne of fraunce

f. v^b   The lawe in the boke of numeri for successy(on)
Queene Isabell dog(hter) to Kinge philip heyre (to) three Kinges dyeing withowt yssue by who(me) Kinge henry claymed

136

APPENDIX II

          brutus Kinge of England devidyd the Kingdome thres
          diverse Kinges of scottes deposyd for lacke of homage

f. vii[a]   Edwarde the first brought Wales to france and subduyed allmost all scottland
          he that wyll fraunce wynne with scotland he must begynne

f. vii[b]   Robert le bruse usurper of scottland willed in his testament, never to breake leage with fraunce and never to kepe peace or promise with the englisshemen

f. viii[a]   he that wille scotland wynne let him with france first begynne
          Malcolyn invaded england. david le bruse invaded england
          Malcolyn Kynge of scottes slayne in the tyme of Kynge William (t)he secunde and david (t)aken in the tyme of edward the thrydde

f. viii[b]   Scottes in fraunce dyd eate men and wom(en) his fleasshe for daynti(es)
          Scottes delyte in lye(ing)
          Scotland a contray barren of pleasure and goodnes
          Fraunce plentiful
          24 duchies in frau(nce)

f. ix[a]   80 populose cuntreys
          103 bisshoprikes
          1000 and moo monasteryes
          An answer to the earle of Westmorland his oration

THE ANNOTATOR

	a wittye sayenge and (th)acte of Cato censorius
	carthage was distryed by cato his incensynge
f. ix^b	Julius desieryd to conq(ue)re brytayne a farre o(ff) rather then pannonia nyegh at ther hande
	‡note yet the autho(rs) good wylle to religi(ous) howses
	Embassadors to fra(nce) for proclamation of wa(r)
	solempne bankett and iustes
	The commission to req(uire) the crowne of fraun(ce) etc.
f. x^a	A sleight aunswer to the embassadours
	A Tonne of tennes balles sent as ys reported
	A restrainte of promotions to straungers
	A gret provisyon for warre
	The dolphyn protector while the Kynge was (f)allen agayne into his infirmytye
f. x^b	A policie of the frenchmen in fayre offers made
	Embassadours of the frenchmen
	An offer of the lady Katheryne and other bas(e) cuntres for peace
	An answer to the embassadours, by the archbisshop of canterbury
f. xi^a	A stowt bisshop of fraunce so in defiaunce of a prince to speke
	The aunswer of the King of englond
f. xi^b	A rede into scotland
	The Kinges mother in lawe governour of the sayed realme in hi(s) absence

138

APPENDIX II

	A letter of the King of england to the french Kynge
f. xii^a	A sleveles aunswer
	A corage stowte of coragiose capitaynes
	A newe treason and soone confessyd and executyd
f. xii^b	An oration of the Kynge to his Kynsmen rebelles that were attaynted and executyd
f. xiii^a	A new conspiracye
	The passage into fraunce
	An assaulte to harflew
f. xiii^b	The frenche Kynge approchid to rescue but he durst not
	A Truce for iii day(es)
	A weake aunswer of the dolphin
	harflew delivered up to the Kynge of England
f. xiv^a	Wynter approchinge the King intendyd to passe to calice thrughe fraunce by lande bycause it shuld not be sayed he fledde away
f. xiv^b	An armye raysed to stopp(e) ther passage and corne distroyed
	A passage called blanchetaque where the straytes were layed
	note the kowardyce of the frenche men
f. xv^a	A forde to passe over not before espyed
	2000 horsemen 1300 archers left with Kinge henrye by sycknes and no mo at his returne. besydes many moo storms of affliction

139

A cryme committyd and if this boke had had one author it wold not have bene noted / nam (opor)tet mendacem esse memorem
mountjoye Kynge at armes sent in defiaunce to Kynge henrye

f. xv^b The place apointed for battayle
lx. M. horsemen of the frenchemen
The englishe souldiers confessyd themselfes and receayvid the sacrame(nt)
The battayle of Ag(in)courte wonne the 2(5) of october 1415

f. xvi^a gret oddes betwene the englisshe armye and the frenche
pryde hadde a fall
The frenche man notethe the nature of the englisshe man

f. xvi^b An oration of ther captayne against the englisshe armye moche coragiose
first affirminge the englisshe armye weake
seconde the defacinge of the bloude
Thrydde the riches of th englisshe campe

f. xvii^a A notable order of Kynge henry his battayle
The inventynge of stakes which now I thinke be morres pykes

f. xvii^b At the end of Kinge henrye his oration h(e) concludethe that engl(and) prayethe for their succes(se)

f. xviii^a A triumphe of the frenchemen before victorye

APPENDIX II

f. xviii[b]	The frenche vawarde discomfytyd The myddell warde beaten of The duke of alaunson slayne The rerewarde of frenchemen ranne awaye withowt order C A cowardlye acte of VI horsemen of fraunc(e)
f. xix[a]	prisoners pitifully slayne an other sckyrmisshe Thanks to god gevin for victorye
f. xix[b]	The castell of Agincour(t) gave name to the batt(ayle) procession from paules to Westminster for the victorye gevin
f. xx[a]	A grave ground square of XV[c] yardes V.M. & viii[c] buryed in iii pittes that place after made a chircheyarde and walled lamentable verses made by the parisians prisoners taken by the englisshemen noble men of fraunce slayne
f. xx[b]	a marvelose nombre of dukes earles lordes and knightes of the frenche armye slayne Some wryte that only(e) XXV englisshmen we(re) slayne but some other saye that V or VI C were slayne
f. xxi[a]	The Kynge ys come saffe from calice to westminster Crosses copes and censors then massy and ryche [*with an erasure*] gret sorrow emonge the frenchmen

THE ANNOTATOR

                new provisyon by the frenche men for warre
                The dolphyn dyed

f. xxi^b   A rode into normandye by T duke of exceter the captayne of harflew
                The frenche men sckyrmisshed with him and had the better, but not conte(nt) folowid so longe that the hadde the worse.
                Sigismunde emperour laboryd an unitie in christen religyon and pe(ace) emonge christen princes
                The emperour recea(ved) on blackeheathe.

f. xxii^a   The emperour had persuaded peace but for a new siege of the frenchmen made to harflew

f. xxii^b   The Kynge persuaded by the emperour not to go in his owne person
                C C saile apoynted for rescue of harflew
                A victory to the engli(sshe)men on the sea
                V^c shippes hulkes and carickes taken and son(k)
                The duke of bedford entered and refresshid harflew

f. xxiii^a The earle of arminacke retorned to parice with a flea in his eare
                divisyon fell agayne emonge the frenchmen
                Charles the dolphin and John duke of burgoyn renuyd old malice
                fraunce in a harde perplexitie
                The duke of bedforde returned from harflew a victor was praised of the emperour

APPENDIX II

f. xxiii^b — The emperour with the Kinge entred league and returnid into Germanye
The duke of burgoyn(e) came to calice to the emperour and the Kynge
duke of burgoyne suspectyd to be untrew to the crowne of frau(nce) for his voyage to calice

f. xxiv^a — A parliament to declare the iniuries of fraunce
A request made for money and shortlye assentyd unto
The duke of bedford governour of the realme durynge tyme of the frenche warres
A victorye on the sea at the furst scowrynge
nobles assemblyd in the Kynges armye

f. xxiv^b — The normaynes frayd at the Kinges comminge sent worde to Charles the fren(ch) Kynge for ayde
Siege to the castell of tonque
Siege to the towne of Caen

f. xxv^a — The pioners cast trenches to undermyne the walles of the towne
The wynninge of caen

f. xxv^b — The castell (of) caen yeldyd
The frencheman(s) power was wea(k) bycause their Kyn(ge's) wit was not str(onge)
The dolphyne gotte his mother('s) treasure to may(n)teyne warre

143

THE ANNOTATOR

f. xxvi^a The quene Isabell stomakyd the matter that hir treasure was taken, and placed therfor John duke of burgoyne in the roome of governour
marke the yssew of cyvyle dissention
(T)he towne of beaux (w)onne and the cytie (o)f lyseaux
(A) noble and notable acte of pytie

f. xxvi^b A free offer of captaynes to submytt themsellf to the Kyng(e)
The normaynes became subiectes to the Kinge of Englan(d)
Argenton rendryd to the Kyng and thes(e) townes folowyng(e)

f. xxvii^a A soore tempeste that blew a broken maste of a caricke over hampton wall
lorde Cobham appre(h)endyd in the marches of Wales by the lorde powes and hanged and burned

f. xxvii^b A daungerose passage over the ryver of Seyne
A siege to roan the cytie in normandye
A skyrmisshe
loviers rendre(d)
Eureux the cyt(ie) taken

f. xxviii^a The capitaynes of roan spoyled ther owne suburbes

f. xxviii^b The lorde of Kyllmayne with XVI^c Irisshe men came to the Kynge
C C and X^M persones (in) Roan at the beseaginge therof
A devise to fav(our) the men of Roan

144

APPENDIX II

	The syege at Ro(an) contynued from lam(mas) to Christmas allm(ost)
f. xxix^a	A pitiuse case dogges rattes cattes and myse eaten
	Kinge henrye his allmes on Christmas day on newe yeares even (t)he people of Roan beganne to relent
f. xxix^b	xii apointed to speake with the Kinge
	a folisshe embassade
	The Kinges answ(er)
f. xxx^a	bellona the goddesse of battayle hathe iii handmaydes blode fyre and famyn
f. xxx^b	A truce of viii day(es) grauntyd them
f. xxxi^a	Articles for deliveraunce of the cytie of roan
f. xxxi^b	dreedfull ['doubtful' *erased*]
	a reservation of holye reliques
f. xxxii^a	a provisyon for buryall of ther dead
f. xxxii^b	philip de valoyes Kynge of fraunce
	luca Italico except(ed) specially as prisone(r)
	Roan yeldyd upon sainct Wolstan's d(ay) and after gotten town(es) and castelles depe caudebec Tornay
f. xxxiii^a	The Kinge entred roan with iiii dukes and earles viii bisshopes (x)vi barons
	The chaplens sange (Qu)is est magnus dn̄s
	The duke of brytayne entred leage with the Kynge
	Townes frely yeldyd and captaynes apointed
f. xxxiv^a	John duke of burgoyne labored a peace
	The place apointed for treacty of peace
	The metynge of bothe partes

THE ANNOTATOR

f. xxxiv^b	This tractie of peace toke no place
f. xxxv^a	An apparant conclusyon of frendship betwene the dolphyn and the duke of burgoyne
	pounthoyse sodenlye taken by englisshe men
	An army laye ii days befor parys and not fought with all
f. xxxv^b	Thus the duchie o(f) Normandye was become englisshe agayne which had ben with holden from the year of our lord(e) 1255 unto this y(eere)
	An other metyng(e) for peace betwee(n) the duke of burgoy(ne) and the dolphin
f. xxxvi^a	The duke of burgoyne kyllyd with a hatchett befor the dolphin presence by a man of the duke of orleaunce whiche revenget his masters deathe
f. xxxvi^b	philip earle charoloys sonne to John duke of burgoyne late slayne who had to wiff michel doughter to the frenche King(e) toke the deathe of his father hevelye
	The obsequie of the duke John of burgo(yne)
	An offer of peace made to our Kinge by the new duke of burgoyne
f. xxxvii^a	a peace with condition (t)hat our Kinge shuld marry the lady Kathe(r)yne daughter of the frenche Kinge and be heir (o)f fraunce after him
f. xxxvii^b	Kinge henry and lady Katheryne maryed the 3 of June

146

APPENDIX II

f. xxxix^b	note the englisshe tryumphes a padde in the straw, peradventur(e) possessions reservid to spirituall men
f. xl^b	Charles the dolp(hin) exceptid from the leage of peace The date of the articles 30 M(ay) 1420 An othe taken to conserve all the articles wryters reprovid
f. xli^a	A confutation by a case in the lawe longe sufferaunce ys no aquitance The title to the crowne of france was claymed to descende by que(en) Isabell ‡An archefoole and a prothodawe A sharpe begynny(ng) against the dolphyn The duke of burgoynes deat(h) layed to his charg(e)
f. xlii^a	note a pedegree
f. xliii^b	A receavinge of two Kinges and two que(nes) into paris A sittinge in paris upon the deathe of d(uke) John A notable Christmas kept in parys by Kinge henrye
f. xliv^a	The armes of England and fraunce in a new coyne callyd the salute quarterlye set The dolphin condemnid for murder and by sentence of parliament bannissed and deprived The earle of armynacke ayded the dolphin

         The Kynge and quene came to London
         Thankes to godd with V dayes processyon
         The quene crownid the xxiiii of februarye
f. xlv^a   The duke of clarence betrayed and slayne
f. xlv^b   A battell at aniow Anno 1412
         It was thought a goodly matter to graunt a XV of the layte, and a dysm(e) of the clergye. The bisshop of winc(hester) lent the Kynge XX^M l.
         a metynge of the Kynge and the frenc(he) Kynge
f. xlvi^a The Kynge of scottes at our Kinges commandment
         The dolphin fled and was callyd in iest the Kynge of burges and berryes
f. xlvi^b henry the Kynge of england his sonne borne at Windsor
         A notable sayeinge of two Kinge henr(ys)
f. xlvii^a A sckyrmisshe at the bisshopes parke
         A reporte after the frenche cronicle
f. xlvii^b The towne of meux taken and spoyled X° Maii 1412
f. xlviii^a The Kinges of englande and fraunce kept ther pentecost at parys
         A gyrde against Engueraut an historiographier, a scholer in parys
f. xlviii^b Kynge henry fell sycke
         a godlye yeldinge unto god his (visitation) of Kinge henrye
f. xlix^a A request and a fatherly love towards the childe of Kynge henry

APPENDIX II

Kinge henrye his request for his wiff
A commaundement for for peace emong themsellfes and for kepinge off prisoners

f. xlix^b duke homfray ys appointed protector of england
The duke of bedfor(d) Regent of fraunc(e)
Kynge henry committethe his soul(e) to god, his love to his frendes his sy(nnes) to the devell his bodye to the yearth
with his vertues and good parties manifold and wonderfull rare
his activitye
his temperance

f. l^a his corage
his pollicye
his bountifulnes

f. l^b diverse opinions of Kynge henry his disea(se) and death
a plurisis was hys death
he raignes ix year(es) v monethes and xxii(i) dayes and lyved not full 38 yeares

The stature of his bodye and order of his buryall
James Kynge of skottes the principal(l) moorner
500 men of arms rode abowte the chariot in black armour
300 holdinge long torches
And so was he brog(hte) from boys de vincens to paris and so to england and westminster

THE ANNOTATOR
HENRY VI

f. i^a   henry the sixte of the age of ix mon(ethes) proclaimed anno 142(2)
duke of exeter governour
duke of bedford regen(t)
duke of glocester protect(or)
preparation for war in fraunce
the frenchemen forsoke (t)he englisshe captaynes after Kinge charles deathe

f. ii^b   the dolphin proclam(ed) himsellf Kinge of fra(nce) by the name of charl(es) the viith

iii

Examination of the Handwriting
by H. T. F. RHODES

THE purpose of this appendix is to compare the undisputed handwriting of William Shakespeare with the annotations, and to see whether it can be held on technical grounds that the notes could have been written by him.

First it is necessary to consider the acknowledged examples of Shakespeare's hand, and to observe their characteristics of design and those of specific type.

Only six specimens of Shakespeare's writing exist. (*a*) The signature on the Deposition in the case of Bellott v. Mountjoy, 11 May, 1612. (*b*) Two signatures attached to the Conveyance and Mortgage of the Blackfriars property, 10 and 11 March, 1613. (*c*) The three signatures on the will, 25 March, 1616. The additional words *By me* are attached to the final signature.

There is a gross deterioration of the writing between 1612 and 1616. The writing of 1612 shows no abnormal characteristics. It is slovenly, but it is written with fair fluency and speed, and it probably corresponds substantially to the normal hand which Shakespeare might have written at a much earlier age. But the signatures of 1613 begin to show degenerative characteristics. They are less fluently written. There is disconnexion, and there is a progressive decline in handwriting skill. This is shown particularly in the *S* and the long *s* of the signature of 10 March, and also in the *h* and the *k* of the signature of 11 March. Allowance must, of course, be made for the unsatisfactory conditions imposed by writing across parchment strips, but this is but a minor contributory cause.

The signatures on the will of 1616 show a still more marked deterioration, which is particularly pronounced in those at the foot of the pages. Disconnexion has greatly increased, the failure in designing is exaggerated, the pen control is erratic, and there are indications of tremor.

The final signature has been more carefully written, but the same indications of laborious handwriting movement and failure of pen control are to be found. In *William* the minuscules are fully connected, but there are indications of poor pen control in the *W* and notably in the first *l*. In *Shakspeare* the disconnexion reappears and the concluding letters of the signature are without formal design.

On the other hand, even these disordered signatures have individual characters which display skill and design equal or even superior to that of the signature of 1612. This is well shown in the *h* and the second *e* of the name in the first will signature, which is the worst, in the *h* of the second will signature, and in the well designed and fluently written *By* preceding the final signature. This seems to rule out the suggestion, which has frequently been made, that the disorder shown in these writings might be due to general ill-health and premature senility.

APPENDIX III

There are, in fact, no indications of senility in the writing. It is disordered, but it remains vigorous.

There are, however, indications consistent with certain physical and mental disorders which influence the design and movement of handwriting. Among them is alcoholism. In the handwriting of sub-acute and even chronic alcoholics, it is quite common to find firmly written and well-designed characters, alternating, if only occasionally, with defective writing movements and pen control. It must be emphasised that these indications are not specific symptoms of alcoholism. They can also be associated with psychotic conditions and with disturbances of the central nervous system; but alcoholism is the most common and consistent cause of them.

There is one important respect in which all the signatures are comparable. The vigorous shading suggests that muscular vitality was maintained while muscular control degenerated. This tends to support the assumption that alcoholism may have been the cause of the degeneration.

Upon this evidence, incomplete though it is, it is possible partially to construct a physiological picture of the writer. He possessed at least normal handwriting skill which had perhaps already begun to degenerate through carelessness in 1612. Between that year and 1616 some serious disorder, probably alcoholic in origin, produced changes in handwriting movement and pen control.

The object of this analysis of Shakespeare's writing has been to show with what reserve the signatures must be used as standards of comparison for the identification of other writing. None of the palaeographic analyses seems to have taken into account the pathology of the signature writing and its bearing upon the palaeographic methods of identification. These methods are inevitably, and quite properly, restricted to the formal characteristics of design, and their adequacy depends upon the existence of normal standards.

It is unnecessary to discuss the fundamentally gothic foundation of the Shakespearian handwriting: deviations from formal gothic forms may prove to be more significant.

The Signature of 1612.

W The gothic fundamentals of the character are determined by the arcade form of the arch connecting the initial and the final strokes. On the other hand, the tendency to simplification comes out in the restriction of the elaborated loops at the beginning and conclusion of the letter.

h Deviation from conventional gothic design in that the body of the character has no shoulder. Customary in current gothic writing.

a A conventional, but anomalous form. It consists of an exaggerated and rather clumsily executed arcade made clockwise to which is added a spurred staff. This is the so-called legal design of the character.

Terminal Character (?) This letter has been classified by Tannenbaum (*The Booke of Sir Thomas More*, New York, 1927) as a *p*. In the present writer's view this classification is unjustified. The determining element in the identification of this character is the upper loop. This is typical of the writer's long *s*,

APPENDIX III

and matches the loops of three other long *ss* in the signatures. It bears little resemblance to the design of the top of the *p*, whether dictated by convention or custom, in contemporary writings.

Signature of 1613 (10 March).

W Blotting obscures the initial design of this letter. It appears to be either an abortive attempt to form the character itself or an unsuccessful preliminary embellishment. As in the case of the *W* of the signature of 1612, there is a dot within the loop terminating the letter which is a conventional embellishment.

ll These are in general similar in design to those of the 1612 signature, but they lie closer together with the loops impinging.

a This is typical of the simpler gothic *a* which most closely approximates to the roman character. The body is open at the top.

m This character shows a deviation from the gothic model since the tail, instead of being carried from right to left under the letter rises and curves from right to left over the letter.

S The fundamental design is precisely that of the 1612 signature, but there is a marked degeneration in pen control. The tail, which should rise above the first curl of the body actually joins it. Heavy and unnecessary pressure has been applied, so that the end of the stroke, instead of tapering is heavily and clumsily shaded.

s This is a simplified deviation from the gothic form and is, in fact, a roman *s*.

Signature of 1613 (11 *March*).

Wm (contraction of Christian name, the *m* being

written above the capital). The *W* has no initial loop or other embellishment. The general design is similar in other respects. The tail of the *m* is very short.

Signature of 1616 (*Will, page* 1). There is great degeneration in design.

S The simplified gothic design without the *s*-shaped centre.

Signature of 1616 (*Will, page* 2). This signature is very disordered particularly at the beginning and the end. The *W* is embellished with a preliminary *v*-like stroke. The design is very poor.

s Approximating the formal gothic. There is a pronounced upper loop of unconventional design. The staff is straight, but with a concluding narrow loop.

Signature of 1616 (*Will, page* 3). Although laboriously written, this signature is better designed.

By Formally gothic in the initial embellishment of the capital *B*, but the character itself is a small *b* gracefully embellished with two spurs. The *y* is conventionally formed, but consists of two parts, a short shaded stroke which joins a delicate crotchet at the top of the staff.

S Approximating a roman design.

h Unlooped.

Contraction. There are contraction signs over the shortened *William* of the signature of 1612 and that on page 2 of the Will. There is a third over *pe* in the signature of 10 March.

The identification of handwriting, as of finger-

APPENDIX III

prints, depends upon an appreciation of configurations of individual characteristics. In the case of fingerprints, identity or non-identity can be demonstrated as a fact because the configurations are invariable. Invariable configurations in this absolute sense do not occur in handwriting.

Individual characteristics which serve to identify handwriting are not associated with formal design. They are in general deviations from formal design. If they can be isolated, they have special significance in the identification of writing. There are some indications in the Shakespearian signatures of this character.

Penhold. The signatures were written with a pen held obliquely and inclined towards the right. This is shown by the maximum shading (thickness) of the oblique strokes made from left to right.

Pen pressure. In all the signatures from 1613 to 1616, pen pressure is unrhythmically applied, there being sudden increases of pressure. Although less marked, this is found also in the writing of 1612, and it may be said to be an individual characteristic of the writer at least at these periods.

Signature of 1612. There are two characteristics in this writing which can properly be described as individual characteristics. The top of the loop in the first *l* of *William* has an angular form (see photograph). It is most improbable that this is a formal design originally related to handwriting training.

The terminal symbol of the signature has an upper loop characteristic of a long *s*. The lower loop is of a type occasionally associated with a *p*. It may well be that the character is a simplification and contraction of an *s* and a *p*. This device would be in general agreement with the writer's tendency to simplify his writing. The use of the long symbol representing an *s* is most unusual at the conclusion of a word.

Signature of 10 *March* 1613. The top of the loop of the first *l* of *William* again shows the angular formation. The *ll* lie close together as if they were a single character.

Will Signature, page 1. The *ll* show no angular formation in the loops, but the characters impinge as in the previous example.

Will Signature, page 2. The *ll* lie very close together and the second loop shows an angular formation less marked than in the previous examples. The long *s* of *Shakespeare* shows a marked angular formation of the loop closely comparable to the previous examples. The *p* is characterised by a heavily shaded crossing stroke which meets the loop of the *s* (see photograph).

Will Signature, page 3. *y* The formation of this letter with two strokes may be an individual characteristic, but there is obviously no evidence of writing habit where only one example is available.

A characteristically heavily shaded stroke joins the upstroke of the letter, but does not cross the staff as in the previous signature.

Conclusions. Although some signs of degeneration are present, the signature of 1612 probably corresponds substantially to the normal handwriting of Shakespeare. The signatures of 1613 show definite signs of degeneration, and those of 1616 a further breakdown in handwriting movement and skill.

APPENDIX III

There exist, however, in all the writings individual characteristics of some significance for the purposes of identification. They are (*a*) the penhold, (*b*) the pronounced but unrhythmic pen pressure, and (*c*) characteristic deviations from formal design notably in the *l*, the *ll*, the terminal *sp*? and the heavily shaded stroke of the *p*. These indications can properly be regarded as *individual* characteristics.

For the annotations in the margins of the edition of Halle's *Chronicle*, as in the case of the Shakespearian signatures, the writing conditions were not satisfactory. The facility and skill in writing movement is greater than that of the signature writings.

The penhold closely corresponds to that used in the signature writings. The pen pressure shows a much higher degree of control. It is, on the other hand, often over-emphasised as in the signature writings, and the sudden releases of pressure, which are so marked a feature of the undisputed writing, are frequently found.

i The letter is in general a heavily shaded downstroke with a negative slope (from left to right). It is invariably dotted and generally with great positional accuracy.

l The angular formation at the top of the loop of the *l* and in the upward loops of other letters appears with great frequency. This characteristic can properly be described as an individual characteristic.

ll The impinging of the loops of the doubled *l* is

of very frequent occurrence. This can also properly be described as an individual characteristic.

a The most common type approximates to the simplest of the gothic designs. It consists essentially of a small body with a positive slope to which is attached a heavily shaded staff with a negative slope.

m The letter is in general harmoniously designed, with heavily shaded strokes. The connexions are usually angular.

S A simplified form of the gothic S wherein a single *c*-like stroke finally turns sharply from right to left crossing the body and projecting slightly beyond it.

h A typical gothic design as currently written with a small loop and indefinite shoulder. It is invariably connected with the letter following.

k Generally unskilfully made and of confused design. An *l*-shaped body with an added stroke or spur is common.

e The letter is most commonly constructed with two ticks sloping from left to right and without connexion. The more conventional form in which the members are joined with an eyelet loop is also common.

p (*a*) A simplified and individual form made with a shaded down stroke and an unshaded up stroke with a heavily shaded diagonal stroke at the top so that the upper part of the letter is in the form of a cross, (*b*) the same with an added stroke at the top leaving the top of the staff and meeting the crossing stroke so as to form an angular enclosure, (*c*) a graceful form with a larger curved loop and curved

APPENDIX III

tail, (*d*) conventional form with straight staff and angular body attached.

r The conventional open *v*-like form is most common.

s The most common form is the conventional heavily shaded down stroke with the wide loop added shaded at the curvature. There is, however, an interesting variant in the use of the long *s* as a terminal. The two examples found are looped at the top joined to the previous letter and made anticlockwise as with an *l* or *b*. The lower part of the character ends with a curved tail which bends from right to left. (See Plate vii.)

The handwriting of the annotations is skilful, and displays good pen control. Its most significant general characteristic is that it is highly simplified in terms of contemporary techniques of design, but it always remains legible. The psychological interpretation of handwriting is at a very elementary stage; but it remains true that simplified handwriting combined with good legibility is almost invariably associated with good and often superior intelligence. It must be added that the converse is not true.

By comparison of the descriptions of the *design* of the questioned and unquestioned writings, the marked differences are evident. In general the *ss* both capital and long, the *h*, the *a* and the persistently undotted *i* of the authentic writing differ in design to a marked degree. Design could not, however, in this case, determine identity or non-identity, and it is, in fact, of very little use in the appreciation of essential similarities or differences.

On the other hand the *individual* characteristics are significant from the point of view of identification, since all are consistent with the undisputed writings, of whatever date, and some are common to all the writings. It is suggestive that these characteristics are persistently found in the annotations. Although not a specific indication of identity, it is significant that the pen-hold and pen pressure are of the same character in the two writings. The angular formation associated with the loops is persistently repeated in the two writings, and is a suggestive indication pointing to identity.

The united form of the *ll* which is also a habit of the two writers is interesting. The mere juxtaposition of doubled letters would not be significant, however frequently it occurred, since it was a conventional practice of some writers of the period to dispose doubled characters in this way. It may well be a detail of design influenced by handwriting training. But in the writings under discussion, there is a persistent tendency actually to run the letters together. It is an individual habit.

The queried terminal (*sp?*) of the 1612 signature is an unorthodox design which can be compared with two terminal *ss* which occur in the annotations (H.iv.f.xxxii, *Infidels*; H.v.f.xii, Henry V, *rebells*). These designs are also unorthodox since it is a most unusual practice to use long *ss* as terminals.

It is also interesting to compare the heavily shaded stroke joining the *s* to the *p* of the third will signature with the comparable movement as shown by the stroke joining the *s* and the *p* in *spake* (H.v.f.xxix) in the notes. The simplified form of the *p*

APPENDIX III

with the heavy crossing stroke but without the enclosure at the top is closely matched by a similar writing movement in a *p* at H.iv.f.xxiii.

To sum up, though it is difficult to make any valid comparison between Shakespeare's known hand and these notes, because of the disparity in quantity, and because of the pronounced change in Shakespeare's hand in his last years, yet certain 'individual characteristics' appear in all his writing; and these characteristics also appear in the annotations. The differences between Shakespeare's hand and the Annotator's are all differences of design, and not such as to prove a difference of authorship. The similarities, which are all 'individual characteristics', are for that reason more significant, and indicate the probability that Shakespeare and the Annotator were the same man; but do not by any means prove it.

iv

Prognosis on a Shakespeare Problem

by A. P. ROSSITER

This study was written in 1941 and published in the *Durham University Journal*, Vol. 33, No. 2, in March 1941. It is now printed in full without alterations, by kind permission of the author and the Editor of the *Durham University Journal*.

A Hall, Hall, giue roome, and foote it Girles,
More light you knaues, and turne the Tables vp!

THE question of what sort of person William Shakespeare 'really' was, though eschewed by modern critics, is not mere romantic irrelevance. It is inevitable that we should want to make that bland first-folio face abide our question; and that wanting is one of the few links between the interests of the scholarly or semi-professional reader and the respectful, but usually bewildered amateur. These are times when the interests of the academic and the general most particularly need drawing together for something more than the *defence* of a common tradition; so that it is a misfortune of war that Mr Alan Keen's discovery of 'several hundred annotations' in the margins of an old black-letter history-book should have received so slight and so passing attention in the press.

The purpose of the following notes is to examine the possible significance of this 'literary find', supposing that the experts agree that Shakespeare did

APPENDIX IV

annotate and use this copy of Halle's *The Union of the two Noble and Illustre Families of Lancastre and York*. They endeavour to explain to moderately informed readers how their views may be altered or clarified; and thus represent the necessary explanations which should be prefixed to any review of a book on this discovery, unless it is intended solely for experts. Throughout, the aim is to put an impartial outline of possibilities before a non-specialist jury, so that anyone sufficiently interested in Shakespeare can form his opinion of the validity of the arguments that experts may offer, and estimate the importance of their conclusions. The different critical points will be considered under numbered headings, the directional significance of the separate notes being briefly summed up in the last.

1. *Authenticity*. No mention has been made of a signature in this book, so we may assume that it holds none. The authenticity of the notes is therefore a matter of inference. They are not (as one paper suggested) 'the first Shakespeare MSS. ever found', for Addition D to the Harleian MS. play of *Sir Thomas More* has a prior claim of long duration; a claim supported by stylistic evidence, as well as by expert palaeography and what is known as 'critical bibliography'.[1]

The only MSS. which can be used, in the first instance, to show that the hand is authentic are the six signatures. These are all late, while Shakespeare's use of Hall would presumably be early (*c*. 1590-8).

[1] See *Shakespeare's Hand in the Play of Sir Thomas More*, by A. W. Pollard and others (C.U.P., 1923), and especially Chapters iii, iv, and v

THE ANNOTATOR

There may be difficulties here, especially over the earlier plays, but that they need not be insuperable may be seen from the work already done on the *More* MS.[1] It will be clearly a convincing point if those peculiarities of letter-forms which have been used in establishing the D hand as Shakespeare's are found to reappear in these notes. The famous 'three pages' in *More* can be used for comparison, but only in the *second* place:[2] in the *first*, evidence for authenticity must rest solely on the fourteen letters that appear in and with the signatures, and most particularly on those which are written in two or more characteristically variant forms. The most important of these are *a*, *k*, *p*, *s*, and, next to them, *e* and *r*. All such evidence will be strengthened if the annotated parts of the chronicle appear in the plays in a form which is dependent on Hall, or Hall in the light of the MS. comment. Such a concurrence, however, cannot by itself prove that the notes are not by some other person who, like Shakespeare, wrote a not-exceptional Secretary hand.

2. *Hall's Book* was accessible to Shakespeare in the second and third editions of 1548 and 1550: the first having been very thoroughly burnt under Queen Mary. It gives a chronicle of English History from the fall of Richard II to Hall's own day, the purpose of these limits being clear from the title.

[1] See *Shakespeare's Handwriting*, by Sir E. Maunde Thompson (O.U.P., 1916), and his essay in the book mentioned above (Cap. iii)

[2] Otherwise the opponents of the D Addition will only re-deny that it is by Shakespeare. The 'fourteen' in the tail of this sentence includes three capitals (B, W, S)

APPENDIX IV

This runs to some 90 words, which may be condensed as follows: The subject is 'the union of Lancaster and York' after 'the continual dissension for the crown' from the time of Henry IV, 'the first author of this division', till that of Henry VIII, 'the indubitate flower and very heir of both the said lineages'.

This gives it a certain form, and one approaching to what seems to be the obvious design of Shakespeare's Histories: the anarchy that resulted (in the long run) from the deposition of Richard II; the fortunes and fall of the usurping House of Lancaster; the rise of the House of York, till Richard III reigns, arch-gangster in a gangsters' paradise; and, finally, the restoration of peace, order, nobility, rightful sovereignty, and all things desirable under the Tudors. Shakespeare's Histories, though commonly taken to be drawn almost exclusively from Holinshed, certainly keep Hall's limits and have his theme for a framework. Excluding *King John* and the very late *Henry VIII*, they make up two linked tetralogies, the historically later one being written first, after which he went back to the causes of the Wars of the Roses. Thus we have two series:

A. *Richard II:* 1 *and* 2 *Henry IV; Henry V.*
B. 1, 2, *and* 3 *Henry VI; Richard III.*

Though A was written later (1595-8-9) it brings history round to just the point where B is about to begin; while B ends with Henry Tudor's prayer for peace, unmistakably glancing at his granddaughter's reign. The series begins with the deposition and murder of a king, and an episcopal curse predicting rebellion and civil wars, and all the dreadful things which keep occurring throughout both sequences as the result of faction and divided claims to the throne.[1]

Though Hall ostensibly starts with Henry IV, his compass and plan are Shakespeare's; and however they may have *intended* them, their works *act like* 'Tudor propaganda'. In addition to this, Hall indulges in overt 'Protestant propaganda' of the sort that Shakespeare omitted in rewriting the old play about King John.[2] But since 'Protestant propaganda' was of necessity 'Supremacy propaganda', this separation of a specifically 'Tudor' element may be misleading, unless 'protestant' is glossed as 'violently anti-papist'. Certainly 'the calamities' ensuing 'from domestical discord and unnatural controversy' are powerfully stressed by both Hall and Shakespeare; and those who have doubted whether there was 'any room in the Elizabethan theatre' for 'topics of political controversy'[3] can be reasonably asked to define their terms, or to explain why limited autocracy should suppress those who sang in tune with it. Had the politically contro-

[1] See Carlisle's speech at *Richard II*, 4.1.155 ff: *I Henry VI* begins with the loss of Henry V's conquests because of faction at home

[2] Though, as Shakespeare's play shows, there was little point in John unless you made him a 'protestant' hero for defying the Pope. The Bastard's too-celebrated speech at the end hardly sums up anything *in the play*: it is too clearly directed at Spain

[3] Sir E. K. Chambers: *William Shakespeare*, i, 67. My point is that any play about a rebellion or civil war was necessarily on a topic of political controversy. And the Elizabethans were inordinately addicted to such plays

APPENDIX IV

versial question of Non-resistance been impermissible, the period of Hall's chronicle could not have been dramatised at all.

3. *Holinshed.* It is incontrovertible that the Histories are (directly or indirectly) indebted to the 1587 reprint of *The Chronicles of England, Scotland and Ireland.*[1] But Raphael Holinshed more nearly resembled a prototype of Mr H. G. Wells than Hall did. He began with Noah's Flood, and though he often copies verbatim from Hall, he remains the chronicler, where Hall tends towards the historian: that is, if we take it that 'History' implies the existence of some discoverable design, some principles, some approach to general 'laws' worth extracting; while 'Chronicle' represents the mere accumulation of fact, appealing only to curiosity or the collector's passion: the work of minds either incapable of profitable generalisation, or content to defer it till the advent of some unborn genius, after the manner of some of our contemporary 'historians'.

Since the plays derive information from Holinshed, and since their whole scope represents a bare fifth of his third volume, it will be important to decide whether Shakespeare annotated Hall *before* or *after* reading the later book. Hall's design is swamped in Holinshed's sprat-crowded sea; so that if Shakespeare read Holinshed *before*, he went to Hall for his framework: if *after*, he went to Holinshed

---

[1] In *I Henry IV*, 1.1, the malpractices of the Welshwomen are not in Hall: nor is the Rood-day mentioned in connexion with Holmedon Hill. But Hall shows up the slip about Mordake being Douglas's son, saying on one page (24) that he was son to 'the governor', and that this governor was Albany

for more data. If he read them together, or had them read together by someone else, further problems appear.

4. *Other Sources*. Hall comes in here, since Holinshed is regarded as the main source: the current view being that the former provided such details as the allusion to York's age in *Richard II*, 5.2.115, which Holinshed did not copy. Stowe's *Annals* (originally *Chronicles of England*, 1580) is taken to be the source for Mowbray's crusading after his banishment; while the deposition-scene is from Berners' *Froissart*. But in the New Cambridge edition of *Richard II*, Professor Dover Wilson has added the results of wider researches, which seem to show that in addition to the sources given above, the play draws on Daniel's *Civil Wars*, the anonymous play *Woodstock*,[1] and also some rather unlikely French Chronicles.

The most important of these is *La Chronique de la Traïson et Mort de Richard Deux roy Dengleterre*, one version of which, *La Chronique de Richard II*, is attributed to Jean Le Beau, a canon of Liège; to which Dover Wilson tentatively adds the related metrical work by Jean Créton, *Histoire du Roy d'Angleterre Richard II*, parts of which give an eye-witness account of the events of 1399.[2]

The cumulative effect of such evidence is to compel us *either* to consider that Shakespeare worked like a historical scholar, and made his Histories by collating authorities, cross-checking, and (in a word)

---

[1] Sometimes called *I Richard II* (Malone Soc. Reprints)
[2] On the authority of Professor Reyher. See New Cambridge Introduction

APPENDIX IV

Research; *or* to assume that someone else had done this first. Professor Dover Wilson accepts the second hypothesis, largely on the evidence of *King John*, and takes it that there was an erudite compiler of historical syntheses in dramatic form whose work Shakespeare adapted in his own free way.

5. '*Old Plays*' *and King John*. The 'old play' origin of the *Henry VI* trilogy is now discredited; but there can be no doubt that *The Troublesome Raigne of John King of England* (printed 1591) is the source of Shakespeare's play. As Professor Nicoll puts it, John's outburst when he learns of the supposed murder of Arthur 'appears to be the only (and it is doubtful) evidence' that Holinshed was used at all. The old play, however, does not stage Holinshed just as it comes; it seems to be the work of a man well versed in history, who sometimes went far afield for his materials. Fauconbridge, the heroic Bastard, seems to derive from some combination of the following

(1) Thomas Neville, an amphibious *Lancastrian* captain, 'bastard son to William Lord Fauconbridge' (Hall); (2) Falcasius or Foukes de Brente, alias Fawkes de Breauté, a soldier of fortune under John, who sacked St. Albans (Matthew Paris and Holinshed); (3) this same person's 'tough' manner of claiming service with the king, as a bastard of fortune (M. Paris); (4) Dunois, the celebrated Bâtard d'Orleans, and *his* 'tough' manner of claiming his paternity; and (5) Holinshed's contribution that 'Philip, a bastard son to King Richard . . . killed the vicount of Limoges, in revenge of his father's death'.

The composer of this engaging character would

seem to have read up the reign of Henry VI (1 and 4), or to have made the very most of a hint from a monkish chronicle (3), besides improving on Holinshed (2 and 5).¹

There is nothing in *The Troublesome Raigne* to make a reasonable man believe that Shakespeare wrote it; so that here we certainly seem to have the work of such a person, as Dover Wilson suspects to be behind *Richard II* – an able maker of historical scenarios, but no poet. Indeed, at the end of his study of the latter play, Dover Wilson suggests that in the Henry IV group the same thing will be seen: viz. Shakespeare working over old plays made by Somebody Else, and acted by the earlier companies before the Lord Chamberlain's came into being.²

At this point the argument splits into two, and one line must be taken first. I shall deal with the contradictions in the handling of history in the plays in Section 6, and postpone the case for believing in old-play sources till later (Section 9).

6. *History and the Histories.* There is, then, a certain trend in modern investigation, tending to show that

---

¹ No. 1 is mentioned in *III Henry VI*. I am not convinced that 'Fauconbridge' is an impossible derivative of 'Fawkes de Brent' (Fuller calls him 'Falco', and the man asks for the pun). But the Dunois story is so like the one in *T.R.* and *K. John* that it is easier to suppose that both tale and name come from Hall (pp. 144 and 301, 1809 reprint from 1548). I should remind the reader that Hall does not touch King John.

² See Dover Wilson's Introduction to *Richard II*, p. lxxvi. I do not see why some plays should not have been rejected as unactable, even in those uncritical days; when they might be sold in MS. to those who thought they could make a stageworthy job of them – or get William to. Penury might conquer even the vanity of an author.

APPENDIX IV

the Histories are built on wide and fairly careful reading. But this seems quite incompatible with the usual notion of the 'royally careless' Shakespeare who worked, as Dryden put it, 'not laboriously but luckily'. This notion rests largely on the best-known plays: the great comedies and tragedies. But even within the Histories it is not hard to find slips and blunders of a kind that no one would expect from a careful, collating, note-taking, comparative reader.

The man who studied authorities with the care apparently indicated by *Richard II* would not be likely to think that Antony Woodville, Lord Rivers who was Lord Scales in his wife's right, was three different people.[1] He would not have made Cambridge in *Henry V* a mean hireling traitor, seeing that his treason sprang directly from the existence of divided rights to the crown, and that he was (as Hall and Holinshed point out) the father of Richard, Duke of York, and grandfather of Edward IV. He would not have made Hotspur (a man two years older than the King) into a chivalrous youth of an age with Prince Hal; nor have made King Henry lament his son's dissipations at a time when that promising boy was but twelve (as Hall expressly states). He might have been more careful not to suggest in one place that Bagot is the Earl of Wiltshire and *executed*, and subsequently to produce him *living* as a sort of king's-evidence; and I imagine he

---

[1] *Richard III*, 2.1.65-7. This might be only Richard's pretty sarcasm at the way the Queen's relations have been advanced, were it not for the fact that this tripartite gentleman has *two* separate entries in the F. text. It can, of course, be argued that this entry is a reviser's blunder. He is, however, correctly named and entitled in Hall (p. 347).

would have been unlikely to convert John of Gaunt from what the Chronicles suggest he was into what we mostly remember him by.[1] In short, the Shakespeare of the Histories does not play the historian's game at all; he is not a scholarly person who is bothered by inaccuracy or minor muddles. He behaves like an artist, and handles history with considerable freedom in major themes, and much carelessness in minor. The methods which produced *Sejanus* and *Catiline*, by 'invading authors like a monarch', are not his. All which is critical commonplace, till it compels us to believe that his historical syntheses of fact were produced by Someone Else.

7. *The Crux.* But all this is blown sky-high if it can be shown that he did study a historian with annotating care. Professor Dover Wilson's 'old plays' become mere academic phantasies. And since *The Troublesome Raigne* is indisputably the source of *King John*, we must infer either (*a*) that Shakespeare wrote it himself in extreme artistic infancy (a wild conjecture, as will be seen from Section 9), or (*b*) that he learnt to work up history by seeing what Mr Else had done with the reign of King John.[2]

With the plays which could be based on Hall, it

---

[1] Dover Wilson traces him to Froissart; but it seems likelier to me that he is an improvement on the plain-spoken patriotism of Woodstock in the old play. The Gaunt of the Chronicles is more nearly a 'turbulent baron'.

[2] The hypothesis that *T.R.* is an imitation of *K. John*, produced for *reading only*, or for provincial acting, is ruled out by the date, and by the points on which it clears up puzzles in Shakespeare. (See later.) It has been attributed to Peele, with *Edward I* (which is generally admitted to be by the same hand). But though George Peele had a knack with pageants, I am unaware that he ever struck anyone as an assiduous scholar.

APPENDIX IV

is not so much the *existence* of authentic annotations that matters; it is their *nature*. Are they scholarly notes, citing other authorities, with cf.'s and vide's (such as 'in ye ffrenshe boke I reade noe such thynge' or 'a lye, as Vmbraticvs shewth, cap. xl') or are they simply guide-lines such as you might make if you had Mr Else's scenario, but weren't quite sure it didn't pervert history (as propagandists will), or didn't miss details of the sort that provided 'good theatre' or gave you a 'line' on character, a gesture, a good phrase? (Such notes would be on points of fact, I suppose: 'a straing starre seen'; 'Ihon ffastolfe kt. a cowherd runneth awaie'; or perhaps they might *nota* or copy a turn of phrase, to help it stick – as 'huggermugger' stuck while Shakespeare was reading North's *Brutus*, and so reappeared in *Hamlet*.)

If the notes are of the former sort, then Shakespeare read scholarly, and the 'old-play' theory is moribund; for by the principle of Occam's Razor, Mr Else is an unnecessary entity apart from Mr Shakespeare. But while we accommodate our imaginations to a Shakespeare of this sort, we must still gape at his inexplicable carelessness; and particularly at the great number of loose ends and contradictions in the Tragedies, mostly of a kind that a careful worker in factual jigsaws *ought* to be incapable of missing. Miss Dorothy Sayers would have eliminated the ground for much factual criticism in *Othello* and *Lear*: both of which seem the work of a man whose sense of detective-story detailed factuality is weak. Bradley keeps showing this, and though he puts it aside with the remark that it wouldn't be noticed on the stage, such methods seem to originate in a different *type* of mind from one capable of pursuing the fortunes of Richard II through three or four chronicles and into a foreign language.

If the notes are mere guide-lines, then the situation is less puzzling. They might support any of the following theories, according to their exact nature: (1) that Shakespeare came to Hall after reading Holinshed, and saw there a framework – a kind of philosophical principle for the unification of chronicle into poetic history; (2) that he did use Mr Else, though with the addition of telling details from history-books (which may or may not include a direct knowledge of Holinshed); or (3) if he *did not*, that all the parallels from recherché chronicles are so much academic moonshine.

(1) will be supported by notes of an 'architectonic' kind: generalisations such as are found in Hall's opening paragraph on the evils of dissension; fact-edged commonplaces such as his moving comment on Jane Shore's old age; allusions to such figures as that of the State as a Microcosm or anthropomorphic organism – as, for example, when Bolingbroke tells Canterbury that 'as it is hard that the head shall not feel when the hand or any other member is grieved or sick, so it is unlike that any displeasure . . . should not happen to you with which we should not taste in part, such vicinity is among members . . .' (*Hall* p. 7; and cf. *I Henry IV*, passim). We might even hope to see Shakespeare's mind reacting to such a comment as this, on Richard II:[1]

---

[1] Cf. perhaps, *Richard III*, 3.4.98 ff. This citation and the

APPENDIX IV

But such is the frail judgement of mortal men, which vilipending and not regarding things present before their eyes, do ever think all things that are to come to have a prosperous success and a delectable sequel.

– or to trace the dramatic point of the Gadshill robbery and re-robbery to Hotspur's sarcasm, 'Behold the heir of the realm is robbed of his right and yet the robber, with his own, will not redeem him' (*Hall*, p. 28; and cf. *I Henry IV*, 1, 1 and 2). (2) will be supported by notes on points of fact. Much variety is possible here; the right sort of note *could* show that what we now trace to Holinshed did not reach Shakespeare direct. Clearly, the more points of plot that are marked in Hall, the less need for Holinshed as main source; while if points of detail are noted in spite of their reappearance in Holinshed, we may be driven to consider the possibility that a dramatisation by Mr Else lay by Shakespeare's elbow as he wrote.[1] Less speculative, there is the possibility of a clearer understanding of character; as, for example, that of Bolingbroke, if Shakespeare took Hall's hint to 'note with a white-stone' that 'this Henry of Lancaster should be thus

next reappear in Holinshed. The point is that in this copy of Hall they may be marked, noted, or otherwise distinguished; whereas with Holinshed we can only hazard guesses that 'this must have struck him', or 'why didn't this?', etc.

[1] This is complicated. But suppose he had *Woodstock* in mind; he would note (in Hall) that Greene was *not* killed in battle, and that there was in fact *no* battle. The mangled history of the old play would thus be revealed by the notes; and since Hall starts later, we could perhaps infer that he was correcting impressions derived from misdramatised Holinshed.

called to the kingdom ... which (i.e., *who*) perchance *never thereof once thought or yet dreamed*.'

Theory (3), that the apparent use of recondite sources is an epiphenomenon, would be supported by notes which show that intelligent and imaginative guesswork which I imagine most people would expect of Shakespeare. If they show a mind working intuitively towards a grasp of the true nature of the people in the varying pageant of history; the things they thought or said, the reasons why they did things; then the parallels in other records, such as the French, are unimportant. In editing *Julius Caesar* the resources of scholarly ingenuity and classical piety have sometimes been taxed to show how Shakespeare and the letters of Cicero take the same view; but since there is no proof that he knew these letters, the parallels are evidence only of his imaginative grasp of 'men in action'; of his understanding, not knowledge or information.[1] Unless there is an echo of some unlikely or effective turn of phrase, all such 'parallels' rest on the assumption that the 'naturally learned' Shakespeare could only proceed like the patient compiler. Yet we only need North's Plutarch to 'help us to follow his methods of working', and we can see that, with one good source, imagination did the rest. If Shakespeare read human nature 'like a book', he needed only one book for the story; the rest 'occurred to him'.

---

[1] Cf. Gibbon, on a 'parallel' between *M. N. Dream* and St. Gregory: 'Shakespeare had never read the poems of Gregory Nazianzen; he was ignorant of the Greek language; but his mother-tongue, the language of nature, is the same in Cappadocia and in Britain' (iii, xxvii)

APPENDIX IV

How else can we 'explain' Caliban? or show in Holinshed 'where Lady Macbeth came from'? trace Lear from Leir? or (with a finger on North) extract *his* Antony, *his* Cleopatra from Plutarch's?

This view, though general among intelligent readers, cannot be assumed against a sufficiency of evidence. Attention may here be called to one place where apparent dependence on an unlikely source can be 'explained away' on the lines I have indicated. In *Richard II* the king compares himself with Christ in these terms:

> Though some of you, with Pilate, wash your hands
> Showing an outward pity; yet you Pilates
> Have here delivered me to my sour cross,
> And water cannot wash away your sin.
> (4.1.239 ff)

Professor Dover Wilson, following Professor Reyher, quotes a striking passage from Créton's poem, where Bolingbroke asks what he shall do with the king, and the lords reply, 'Nous voulons qu'il soit mené a Westmoustier'; when the poet recalls Christ before Pilate, the Jews' reply, 'Nous voulons qu'il soit crucifié', and Pilate's washing his hands and saying, 'Je suis innocent du sanc juste'.

But both authorities[1] also quote Holinshed's comment on the rebellious Archbishop of Canterbury: 'he prophesied not as a prelat, but as a Pilat'; a hint which seems to me to supply the whole figure, if we reflect how familiar to the Elizabethans

[1] Neither of the Professors seems to recollect the Second Murderer's allusion in *Richard III*, 1.4.279

was the staged spectacle of a sacrificial king of sorrows before the judges. The York Mysteries were performed till 1579, the Chester till about 1600, the Beverley as late as 1604; and all hurt their audiences with

> A sight most pitiful in the meanest wretch,
> Past speaking of in a king.

8. *Difficulties.* There are, however, points of fact in the Histories which could hardly 'occur' to anyone who was guessing. In *Richard II*, Mowbray is said to have died at Venice after fighting 'for Jesu Christ in glorious christian field'. Holinshed, repeating Hall verbatim, says that he went to Germany and then to Venice, 'where he for thought and melancholie deceassed'. Even Sherlock Holmes could not deduce a crusade from this; so we are left wondering whether the detail came from Stowe, who says that Mowbray's death was 'after his return from Jerusalem', or from the French chronicle, in which Mowbray is given permission to go among the Saracens and unbelievers if he will. Again, the English chroniclers say that the Bishop of Carlisle was given to the charge of the Abbot of Westminster. Since Le Beau *implies* that the latter went bail for him later, it seems legitimate to argue (with Dover Wilson) that this detail came from the French;[1] otherwise, why depart from Holinshed?

---

[1] Dover Wilson's note on the passage (iv.i.152-3) is incorrect in saying that 'Hall, Holinshed, and *Traïson* state that Carlisle is consigned to the charge of the Abbot of St. Albans'. The first two say, 'committed to ward in the abbeie of saint Albon(e)s'. After this Carlisle appears, one page later in Hall, two in Holinshed, as a member of the Abbot of Westminster's

APPENDIX IV

Such instances may not be numerous; but taken with the evidences of reading the English chronicles back and forward, they strengthen the case for a careful compiler, who worked from a variety of different sources.

9. *Other Historical Puzzles*. While a Shakespeare with a collector's passion for old odd ends of history *may* explain their presence, there are certain incoherent details which are far more easily attributed to his use of 'old plays'. In *Richard II*, 2.1, the list of rebel gentlemen seems to come from Holinshed, though the names are a trifle muddled; but the phrase 'that late broke from the Earl of Exeter' does not relate to Cobham (as would appear), but to the young Arundel, Canterbury's nephew. It comes from two pages earlier in Holinshed;[1] so that although the text is faulty, the writer's intention is clearly to bring in a detail he had noticed in reading, though before he could have considered Arundel important.

Against this may be set two lapses. Hall and

plot. I am not sure that Dover Wilson's point could not be met by saying that a reader might naturally infer that, since Carlisle got into the plot, the *abbey* was accessible to, or within the jurisdiction of, the other Abbot. The alternative is to suppose that *someone* read *both* French chronicles, and preferred Le Beau.

[1] Richard II, 2.1.280 ff. '*His* brother' must refer to Richard, Earl of Arundel; but the text leaves you guessing between Exeter and Cobham. Malone supplied a line: 'The son of Richard, Earl of Arundel' between 'Cobham' and 'That late broke . . . etc.' I think that 'The *heir* to Richard, Earl of Arundel' would make 'his brother' follow rather more naturally. But that some such line must be supplied is obvious.

Holinshed give circumstantial accounts of how Richard stopped Bolingbroke from marrying the daughter of the Duke de Berry; but Shakespeare's allusion to 'the prevention of poor Bolingbroke about his marriage' is left quite unexplained: the chief sufferer never mentions it. Throughout the play the important question of Woodstock's murder is left intolerably obscure, though the opening scenes lose much point unless we know that Richard connived at it with Mowbray as his agent, and that Bolingbroke either knows or strongly suspects this.[1]

Such instances of the absence of required explanation and the presence of needless or confusing detail might be multiplied. It is true that it was Henry's 'trusty brother-in-law' who managed the plot to kill him at Oxford (*Richard II*, 5.8.137); but apart from this one allusion John Holland, Duke of Exeter (demoted) and Earl of Huntingdon, does not appear in the play. Yet against this love of 'merely corroborative detail' there are such apparent lapses as the failure to give any hint that the York who dies so decoratively at Agincourt was in fact the Aumerle (demoted to Rutland) of the earlier play, or that Bedford was 'that same sober-blooded boy' John of Lancaster, in *II Henry IV*. In one place ineffectual detail is

[1] This is in Holinshed (iii, 489) but not in Hall. It does not seem to me easy to suppose that the audience knew these things, or that they were expected to remember them from *Woodstock*. The hashed history at the end of that play makes it impossible to regard it as a 'Part I' to Shakespeare; and in any case the Governor of Calais who has Woodstock murdered is there called Lapoole, not Mowbray.

APPENDIX IV

dramatised: in another, what could be effective is not.[1]

Now on the evidence from *King John* such puzzles can be explained as one of the effects of using 'old-play' materials. Referring to *The Troublesome Raigne*, we can see at once why Shakespeare gives us a motivelessly murderous monk, and a Bastard who is inexplicably derisive about the Dauphin's courtly-love-making and the fidelity of Austria's hypothetical wife. In *King John* none of these things make sense; but in the old play we see abbeys being pillaged, and Simeon vowing murder and martyrdom; we see the Bastard cheated of his bride, Blanche, whom political considerations hand over to the Dauphin. Thus Falconbridge's threat to make a cuckold of *Austria* refers, really, we might say, to the Dauphin *in the other play*!

A writer conscientious about historical detail would not do such things: one working up material from Holinshed need never blunder into them; but in *King John* we can not only see that they have happened, we can easily recognise *how they came about*. When we observe the same phenomena in other plays, we may think it reasonable to attribute them to the same cause; the working-over of ready-

---

[1] Perhaps only a question of taste. But Shakespeare seems to be quite interested in Lord John when he is 'sacked' by Falstaff; so that his four speechless appearances (out of six!) and his mere seven lines make me think that 'Bedford' was a vox nihili to Shakespeare when he wrote *Henry V*. (Cf. Dover Wilson's plausible suggestion that in *King John* Shakespeare confuses King and Dauphin, apparently on account of a vague impression that all French kings ought to be called Louis.)

made plays by a man who was no hand at detective-story detail, and very little interested in historical correctitude.[1]

(Here the reader may be referred back to Section 7 again.)

10. *A Summing Up*. The chief points raised by this discovery have been outlined, with a conspectus of needful data: it remains to suggest directions, which are not 'directions to the jury'. Indeed, where I have lapsed from impartiality in showing how critical contentions might be met, I would wish to prefix to each point the judicial formula: 'You have heard it argued, gentlemen, and you may find that argument satisfying. . . .' Certain major points can, however, be restated without laying down the law.

We may look to these Hall-annotations for a view of Shakespeare as a reader: a valuable aspect of any mind. We may see a little of how history was transmuted to poetic history; and perhaps, too, his reasons for accepting Hall's time-limits and some of his limitations.[2] The scholarly may try to re-

[1] i.e., the needless exactitudes are not his. But in *King John*, 4.2.120 he says Elinor died on April 1, which is true; but it is not in *T.R.*, nor in the chronicles. I mention the point to show that here again we can find evidence of what can be made to look like abstruse research. Holinshed records what sounds like an aurora on this date, and Elinor's death is on the same page (iii, 167); and possibly this explains how Shakespeare(?) won at the odds – 364 to 1 against. With regard to Constance's death, his 'three days' should be multiplied by 365. The scene thus leaps nimbly from 1204 back to 1201, reaches 1212 a dozen lines later, and proceeds to 1216!

[2] Those of 'Tudor propaganda'. Modern histories do not support Hall's view of the dreadfulness of the Wars of the

estimate his debt to Holinshed; perhaps with conversion in view. All these directions depend on the *nature* of the notes; their *existence* proves only that he read Hall; perhaps *after completing* the Histories.

If the notes are scholarly, including additions and corrections, we may have to re-envisage Shakespeare: puzzled the more by his lapses, his empty hints and exact irrelevancies. We may inquire, perhaps, whether his sense of the importance of casual fact weakened with time; whether Aristotle's famous distinction between historic and poetic 'truth' sprang into his amazing intuition, and made him 'careless'. If he was unscholarly, we must suspect certain researchers of going the longest way round to show that he was like a god in his apprehension of men. We may speculate whether he had more or less than Hall plus Holinshed to work on; and whether that more or less was the historical compilation of another man, a wide and intelligent reader, with some sense of 'the drama of history', who netted fish which Shakespeare transformed into men. If not, we are left to explain the myriad-fact-struck mind which would seem to have been 'a very Antony', equally devoted to and defeated by the infinite variety of his lined and treacherous charmer.

Roses to all Englishmen. But this view was exactly what the Tudors – naturally and wisely – wanted 'put across', because of the threat from Spain, as well as their own security.

V

A Model for Malvolio

by BEATRICE LILLEY

IN April 1932 Professor Alwin Thaler, of the Department of English, Tenessee University, published a thesis, 'The Original Malvolio?' in the *Shakespeare Association Bulletin* (Vol. vii, No. 2).

I think I have found the original Malvolio [he wrote] or at least a personage who looks more like the living model from whom Shakespeare might have drawn than any yet suggested. I believe that this model – for the *man* Malvolio, not necessarily for nice details of the episodes in which he is concerned – was William Ffarington, Esq. (1537-1610), of Worden, Lancashire, steward (until 1594) to Ferdinando Strange, Earl of Derby and patron of Shakespeare's company.

In fact, Thaler goes further and extends this origin to Shakespeare's other noteworthy steward, Oswald, in King Lear.

Malvolio and Oswald are, as it were, two lodged together. . . . The fact that these two, almost the only Shakespearian stewards worth mentioning, appear to be two of a kind whom Shakespeare disliked heartily, would seem to establish some preliminary ground for the hypothesis that he drew them from some living model whom he thought worthy to be remembered.

APPENDIX V

We know, of course, that others before Thaler had searched for an original from whom Shakespeare might have drawn Malvolio. Sir Edmund Chambers identified him as Sir William Knollys, the Comptroller of the Royal Household. Gollancz[1] thought he recognised him in 'Sir Ambrose Willoughby, Queen Elizabeth's Chief Sewer and Squire of the Person'. Thaler thinks they 'looked too high' and makes the following observation:

> Shakespeare certainly kept his eyes open at Court as well as elsewhere and used directly or indirectly, much of what he saw there. Yet it does not follow that he put into his plays nearly so many full-length portraits or great persons as some enthusiasts would have us believe. . . . Shakespeare, for many good reasons, is less likely to have modelled his characters upon princes, potentates and powers than, like Mark Twain, upon his uncles, his cousins and his aunts, or rather, like Chaucer, upon his personal and professional associates, neighbors and acquaintances. I am confident, therefore, that in seeking the original Malvolio among Shakespeare's quasi-associates I am at least pointing in the right direction. . . .

Indeed, he was. Let us consider the history and personality of the important Mr Ffarington. Thaler's deductions had been inspired chiefly by the character of Ffarington as he reveals himself in the *Derby Household Books* (of which, as steward, he was the author) and from the portrait given to us by Canon Raines, editor of the *Derby Household Books* in 1853:

[1] *A Book of Homage to Shakespeare*, pp. 177-8

Ffarington as Raines has shown us [writes Thaler] was born in 1537 and inherited from his father, Sir Henry Ffarington, a large property, an official connection with the Stanley family, an inordinate 'appetite for law' and nice conduct as a public official (and) an authoritative and unyielding manner which his inferiors and even 'the surrounding gentry . . . felt . . . sometimes to be inconvenient . . . and at other times oppressive.' He increased his property by a prudent marriage to a wealthy young daughter of the house of Stanley and by shrewd legal management. Meanwhile, he had become a Justice of the Peace of his home County and comptroller of the household to Edward, Earl of Derby.

During the years between 1572-1594 he acquired lands, rebuilt his ancestral seat, 'sought confirmation of the heraldic honours of his family', lent money to his neighbours, settled disputes and (like Malvolio) busied himself with 'arguments of state' ranging all the way from the putting down of May games to the raising of local funds to support the wars.

Raines continues the sketch:

The salient points of character are vividly marked and fully before us . . . that he was not often found at Whitsun Ales or Wakes of Leyland and that the pastoral days of pipe and crook and dance and song were little heeded by him. That he entered not with much spirit into the theatrical representations at Knowsley and New Parke . . . that he had not much delight in comic humour or a particle of imagination or sentiment or romance about him may be readily admitted. His life was that of a prosperous man . . . practi-

APPENDIX V

cal and cautious, the mind always on the stretch and the affections perhaps not much in request.

He completes the picture with his description of Ffarington's portrait at Worden Hall:

> His features are handsome and regular; face somewhat square, eyes dark, complexion florid, forehead high ... lines across it indicative of thought ... beard thin, peaked, slightly gray. He wears a russet coloured doublet, free from the fashionable 'slashing and jagging' at that period so much affected, also a sable fur across his shoulders and a large chain of linked gold in three rounds across his chest. In his right hand he holds a silver-headed cane or it may be a wand of office. He wears the monstrous double cambric ruff stiffened or wired, being (according to Stubbs in *The Anatomy of Abuses*) set three or four times double and of some fitly called three steps and a half to the gallows ... and he wears a ring on his little finger, in his left hand a scented glove embroidered with gold, on his forefinger a signet ring. ...

Thaler observes that other gentlemen too, of course, wore the double ruff, but points out that 'few of them all, surely, had anything like Ffarington's personal and professional qualifications as a proper model for Malvolio and Oswald.'

Ffarington's own records make it abundantly clear that he had little patience with plays or players. In an earlier thesis[1] Thaler has called attention to the fact that during the two or three

---

[1] *Faire Em (and Shakespeare's Company?) in Lancashire.* Reprinted from the publications of the Modern Language Association of America, Vol. xlvi, No. 3, September 1931.

years (1587-90) actually covered by the *Derby Household Books* Ffarington names even the least of the many household guests but fails to name even one of the thirteen plays by at least four different companies whose appearances at the Lancashire residences of the Stanleys he records in his 'fragmentary' entries for this period. In most cases he says no more than, 'Plaiers played', or 'Plaiers wente awaie'.

The household rules he instigated on his inauguration as steward in 1572 (and recorded by himself) show that he would have exterminated entirely, had it been possible, such tiresome inconveniences as 'doggs', 'boys', 'slaves' and 'vagrants'. And doubtless in this latter category he also classed 'plaiers'.

His pedestrian mind and monumental lack of imagination reduced events to incidents, so that all we are told of the birth of Lord Strange's daughter (for instance) is that 'On Mondaie the Mydwiffe came' and, two months later, 'Wednesdaie was the crystening of my L. Strange's daughter'. A fire which threatened to destroy the house at Lathom stirred him to no other comment than 'This night fyre begune in the Buttre'. A state banquet meant no more to him than 'Mondaie many at din(ner)' and in his eyes only such dignitaries of the household as 'Mr Comptrowler', 'Mr Receyver Generall' and (of course) 'Mr Steward of the Howsehold', deserved a name. Small wonder, then, that players were mentioned only occasionally and always anonymously.

Now this side of Ffarington [writes Thaler], his unimaginative self-righteousness as a man, his

APPENDIX V

'superserviceable' devotion to his principals, his surliness towards servants and his instinctive distaste for players – is something of which Shakespeare may well have seen and heard something . . . Shakespeare might have remembered him for many reasons. Perhaps it was merely because Ffarington was no lover of players in general; possibly some particular coldness on Ffarington's part towards Shakespeare's company was the more warmly remembered by them. Certainly it is hard to believe that a character and personality so strongly marked as that of Ffarington as he reveals himself in his writings could have failed to attract Shakespeare's notice if he knew of him at all . . . a man of ability and substance but one marked among multitudes by an abysmal lack of humor and his profound dislike of cakes and ale, especially for the *hoi polloi*. He was well-born and he achieved honors and distinction by his own efforts. His pride of place is understandable but his colossal self-importance would have been no less trying to his inferiors. Though he privately gave alms on occasion to the poor and humble the players would have noticed his painstaking – not to say niggardly – frugality, personal and official. They could not have been unaware of his stubborn integrity but while he lorded it over them they, his superiors in all the man-becoming graces, must have ached to caricature his obstreperous litigiousness, his 'neat' and grave pomposity, his lurking vanity and his unsmiling ambition . . . . He ought to be the great original even if he is not.

A strong case, argued convincingly. But Thaler is forced to admit that 'Ffarington's claims must rest, finally, not upon certainties but upon comparative probabilities'. He has no evidence that Shakespeare did visit the Derby household during the term of Ffarington's stewardship. It has remained for Chance and the passage of two decades to supply the truth that eluded him; which, had he known it, lay in one of Ffarington's entries, as we shall see.

In searching to establish the probability of Shakespeare's having visited Knowsley (or the Derby Lancashire residences) during the years of Ffarington's stewardship Thaler could base his assumption only on the knowledge available to him that by the year 1590 Shakespeare had joined Lord Strange's Players. We know that Ffarington's stewardship ended in 1594; therefore (Thaler must have reasoned) if the two had met at all it must have been between the year that Shakespeare joined Strange's men and the end of Ffarington's term of office. Thaler's twofold reason for believing they did meet during these four years is sound:

(1) The Stanleys loved plays and their company (Strange's) is known to have been at Coventry, Shrewsbury, Leicester and perhaps at the nearby Chester, that is to say, within easy range of its patron's Lancashire residences, year after year between 1591-1594. (I cannot prove, to be sure, that Shakespeare was among the visiting players. The chances are, however, that his interest in travelling players – *vide* Hamlet – was not altogether academic or impersonal. Sooner or later few of the tragedians of the city, beginners or masters, escaped the necessity of travelling 'on the hard hoof'. It is virtually certain at any rate

APPENDIX V

that among the visiting players in Lancashire during these years were such men as Kemp and Edward Alleyn, Augustine Phillips and John Heminges, Shakespeare's fellows and formerly of Leicester's men or the Queen's or Strange's. In other words, it is at least almost certain that Ffarington was a character well known to the players.)

(2) If Shakespeare's company did play in Lancashire during these years it was merely living up to its traditions; for I think I have shown in the earlier study already referred to[1] that Strange's Men may be traced in Ffarington's domain at Knowsley or Lathom or New Parke about 1589-1590 and that there is reason to believe that this company stood lowest of them all in the steward's good graces. I may recall here that these inferences rest upon two sets of facts. First, as a group of Ffarington's own entries (four in all between Christmas 1587 and February 1590) concerning a company of which he disposes summarily as '*the* Plaiers'. Since Ffarington invariably refused to signify those more or less immediately under his thumb by naming them I take this company to be that of the household, Lord Strange's Men. In the second place this interpretation is confirmed and the presence of Strange's Men in one of the Stanley houses about 1590 – probably soon after Shakespeare had joined the company – is virtually attested by two passages in the comedy of *Faire Em*, a Strange's play dating between 1589-1591. These passages, which could hardly have been intelligible to any but a Lancashire audience,

[1] *Faire Em (and Shakespeare's Company?) in Lancashire*

contain two outspoken compliments to Sir Edmund Trafford, an important associate and friend of the Stanleys who is thrice mentioned in Ffarington's record for 1587-1589 as a household guest of the family while the players were acting.

We see that Thaler has made a special note of Ffarington's four entries concerning 'the Plaiers' between Christmas 1587 and February 1590. Elsewhere in his thesis he quotes another for the week ending 30 December 1587: 'Sir Thomas Hesketh; players wente awaie.' As we have seen (p. 47), that entry should read simply: 'On Saturday Sir Thomas Hesketh players wente awaie.'

We believe that Shakespeare joined the Hesketh Players at Rufford in 1585; during Christmas two years later (as Ffarington has shown us) the Hesketh Players visited Knowsley. Here was the fact that eluded Thaler – that Shakespeare visited Knowsley as a player during the years of Ffarington's stewardship.

vi

Alexander Aspinall

IN the Commonplace Book of Sir Francis Fane, of Fulbeck, the dramatist who died about the year 1689, occurs the entry:

> The gift is small, the will is all,
>   Asheyander Asbenall.
> Shaxpaire upon a paire of gloves
> that mas(t)er sent to his mistris.

'Asheyander Asbenall' is Alexander Aspinall, Master of Arts of Brasenose College, Oxford, who became master at the Grammar School, Stratford-on-Avon, in 1582 and there continued over forty years. Fripp[1] writes that Aspinall in later life 'betrothed himself to Widow Shaw the neighbour of the Shakespeares in Henley Street, widow of the late Rafe Shaw whose goods John Shakespeare inventoried in August 1582, and mother of Shakespeare's friend and overseer of his will, Julius Shaw.' Master Aspinall made her the customary gift of a pair of gloves, which apparently he purchased at John Shakespeare's shop, for with them was sent a posy by William Shakespeare to this effect:

> The Gift is small, the Will is all
>   Alexander Aspinall.

The 28th October 1594, a Monday, was Master

[1] Edgar I. Fripp, *Shakespeare, Man and Artist* (Oxford 1938)

Aspinall's wedding day, with the entry in the Register:

Alexander Aspynall & Anne Shaw

and the couple settled in the Chapel Quad, a few yards from New Place. Stopes[1] observes that 'this master became more identified with the School and the Town than any other. Though his relation to Shakespeare could not have been magisterial, he was probably a friend, certainly an acquaintance...'

During Aspinall's tenure of office, on 14th February 1595-6, it was resolved by the Bailiff and a number of the School company, *'that there shall be no School kept in the Chapel from this time following.'* There is a curious allusion to the practice – and possibly to Aspinall – in *Twelfth Night* (3.2).

> Most villainously, like a pedant that keeps
> a school in the church.

Both Stopes and Fripp have written about this Stratford worthy, chiefly from township records. It was, however, his Lancashire surname that aroused my curiosity. Aspinall was connected with the family of Alexander Houghton, and thereby with those of Hesketh, Nowell and Towneley.

Sir Thomas Hesketh had two great houses – at Rufford and at Martholme, the latter being the manor-house of Great Harwood, and his favourite residence, which he rebuilt in 1561. This mansion was adjacent to Read Hall, the seat of the Nowells, the two parks being only separated by the River Calder. The Heskeths and Nowells were close in kinship.

---

[1] C. C. Stopes, *Shakespeare's Warwickshire Contemporaries*

APPENDIX VI

Robert Nowell, of Read Hall, the brother of Dean Alexander Nowell, was a generous gentleman. Grosart,[1] the editor of the accounts of his monetary disbursements points, not without decorous excitement, to such names as Edmund Spenser and Richard Hakluyt, as being recipients of Robert Nowell's bounty.

But we are concerned with another name – Alexander Aspinall – and the entry on page 124 of the Nowell MS.

> Too one Alexander Aspinall, a poore
> scholer, the XXV° of October. Ao. 1572
> at the sute of Brasynoose . . . Xiijs.iijd.

Here is our man! Nineteen years of age and a 'poor scholar' of Brasenose.

Once launched, Aspinall took his B.A. on 25th February 1574/5, and M.A. on 12th June 1578, and, we assume, returned to his home at Standen near Clitheroe in Lancashire.[2] That he then visited his benefactor and family connexions is likely; but could Alexander Aspinall have known the young 'Shakeshafte' in Lancashire, as we know he did in the later years at Stratford when the 'pedant who kept a school in the church' lived within a stone's throw of New Place, where the now prosperous William Shakespeare dwelt?

I suggest that Aspinall could have known 'Shakeshafte' in Lancashire between 1578 and 1581.

---

[1] *The Towneley Hall MSS. The Spending of the Money of Robert Nowell of Reade Hall, Lancashire.* Edited by the Rev. Alexander Grosart (printed for private circulation, 1877).

[2] Alexander Aspinall in the Matriculation Book of Brasenose is described as 'of Lancashire'

It was about 1578, we believe, that Shakespeare went to join the household of Alexander Houghton at Lea, and it was in that year that Aspinall returned to Lancashire, *in artibus magister*. Now, it is even possible to surmise that Aspinall also entered the Houghton household, as a tutor to Alexander Houghton's singing boys.

In the autumn of 1581 Shakespeare returned to Stratford, and in November of the following year married Anne Hathaway. That year Alexander Aspinall also came from Lancashire to succeed John Cottam, another Lancashire man, and a papist as we have seen, as Master of the Grammar School. Shakespeare probably remained in or around Stratford until 1585, when he moved to Rufford Old Hall to enter the employment of Sir Thomas Hesketh.

Perhaps Aspinall urged him to follow up the commendation of Alexander Houghton; perhaps Shakespeare took with him introductions from the schoolmaster to Lancashire friends.

It may have been in gratitude for this, or for early tuition at Lea, that Shakespeare, home at Henley Street on a visit from London nine years later, graced his father's sale of gloves to the ageing lover with the doggerel posy.

vii

A Note on the Frontispiece

IN the John Rylands Library, Manchester, hangs the portrait of a young man, Shakespeare's exact contemporary. It was noticed in 1907 at Winston-on-Tees, near Darlington, and purchased by Thomas Kay, who presented it to the Rylands Library. It is painted on an oak panel. The portrait is inscribed with an age exactly corresponding to Shakespeare's, 'AE SVAE 24, 1588', and the face has certain resemblances to the Droeshout portrait. The picture is known as 'the Grafton portrait' because until 1876 it was for many generations in the possession of the Ludgate family at Grafton Regis, Northants.

It was reproduced by Professor Dover Wilson as the frontispiece to *The Essential Shakespeare*, and the editors of Dr John Smart's posthumous *Shakespeare Truth and Tradition* used it likewise. Dover Wilson says that Dr Smart, 'the sanest of modern Shakespearian biographers, "found in it his own idea of the youthful Shakespeare, and wished it genuine".'

Thomas Kay published a book on his theory that the portrait was in fact of William Shakespeare; and included a fanciful account of the sacking of the Great House at Grafton Regis by Cromwell's troops, suggesting that the portrait was carried off with the spoil.[1]

This may or may not have happened; probably not; for if the portrait *is* of Shakespeare, it is not difficult to explain how it originally came to the neighbourhood of Grafton.

Shakespeare's daughter Susannah married John Hall, and they had one child, Elizabeth. Shakespeare died when she was nine, and left her the reversion of all his estate on the death of his wife and his sister Joan. Elizabeth lived with her parents at New Place, Stratford-on-Avon, from 1616 until her marriage at nineteen to Thomas Nash, also of Stratford. In 1646 her husband died, leaving her childless. Two years later Elizabeth married John Barnard, who had an estate at Abington, Northants; and Abington is only nine miles from Grafton Regis.

Elizabeth's husband was knighted by Charles II in 1661. She died, childless, in her sixty-fourth year, and is buried at Abington. It is quite likely that, as Shakespeare's ultimate heiress, she would have brought with her a portrait of her grandfather when she came to live at Abington Hall. After her death, and that of her husband four years later, anything may have happened to it. The next occupant of the Hall, Anne Thursby, may have sold it or given it away locally.

Now, however, we can put forward an alternative connexion which lands the portrait even closer to Grafton Regis.

As we have noticed, the year of the portrait was

[1] Thomas Kay, *The Story of the Grafton Portrait of William Shakespeare* (Partridge 1914)

APPENDIX VII

also that of Sir Thomas Hesketh's death; which we take to be Shakespeare's last year in residence at Rufford. The Fermor-Heskeths later moved their principal residence from Rufford to Easton Neston, the home of the present Lord Hesketh. And Easton Neston is only *four* miles from Grafton Regis.

We know that the young Shakespeare (or Shakeshafte) was a sufficiently striking personality to have earned special commendation from his first master. Very possibly in the Hesketh household he likewise gained affection and respect; and so his new employer may have commissioned a visiting artist to do a portrait of him. This picture would then have become a possession of the Heskeths, and have travelled with them to Easton Neston.

Another gossamer thread of coincidence which clings to Easton Neston is the story that a solicitor in the nearby town of Towcester remembered seeing, shortly before the war, the name Shakeshafte in some old title-deeds. And in one of them, the name had been changed to Shakespeare.

viii

Shropshire

TWO EPITAPHS

In Tong Church, Shropshire, are the tombs of Sir Thomas and Sir Edward Stanley, bearing poetical epitaphs engraved at their ends. Sir Thomas was of Winwick, Lancashire, and died in 1576. His widow, who died in 1596, had been Margaret Vernon, of the famous Shropshire family. Sir Edward was a brother of Henry, fourth Earl of Derby, and his frequent visits to Knowsley and Lathom between the years 1561 and 1589 are recorded in the Household Books. He died in 1609.

These epitaphs are described, and attributed to Shakespeare, in a MS. of *c.* 1630. It is reproduced in facsimile by Halliwell-Phillips in his *Folio* of 1853, and more fully described by him in *Reliques*, p. 32. Later it was at Warwick Castle.

This MS. seems to be an earlier authority than Sir William Dugdale, who copied one epitaph with slightly different punctuation and spelling, in a collection appended to his *Visitation of Shropshire*, 1664. Thence Sir Isaac Heard, Garter, gave it to Malone, who printed it.

Halliday thinks the epitaph on Sir Edward sounds as if it might be by Shakespeare, but not that upon Sir Thomas. We agree with this, and of course hold that Shakespeare is likely to have met

APPENDIX VIII

Sir Edward at Knowsley, either when the poet was there with Hesketh's Players, or when he first started work with Strange's Men. Sir Edward was Lord Strange's uncle.

Here are the epitaphs, as quoted in the Halliwell-Phillips MS.:

Shakespeare. An epitaph on Sr. Edward Standly Ingraven on his Tombe in Tong Church.

> Not monumentall stones preserves our fame:
> Nor sky-aspiring Piramides our name:
> The memory of him for whom this standes
> Shall outlive marble and defacers hands
>> When all to times consumption shall be given
>> Standly for whom this stands shall stand in Heaven.

On Sir Thomas Standly.

> Idem, ibidem
> Ask who lies heere but doe not wheepe;
> Hee is not deade; hee doth but sleepe;
> This stony Register is for his bones,
> His Fame is more perpetuall, then these stones,
>> And his own goodnesse with him selfe being gone,
>> Shall live when Earthly monument is nonne.

NEW PLACE DOCUMENTS

In 1886 there came to light the purchaser's and vendor's exemplifications concerning New Place, Stratford-on-Avon, 1597 – the year that Shakespeare acquired the house. These papers were found among the papers of the Severne family, of Wallop Hall, Shropshire.

THE ANNOTATOR

Thomas Severne of Broadway and Powyck, Worcestershire (d. 1592), married in 1587 Elizabeth, daughter of John Nash of Martley, Worcestershire. If hence there sprang a family connexion between the Severnes and the John Nash mentioned in Shakespeare's will, it is easy to see how these papers of his came to be at Wallop.

ix
Lancashire
LOCAL WORDS

A LIST of words used in the vernacular of South Lancashire and also by Shakespeare:

Barn	*Child*
Coil	*Stir*
Giglet	*Wanton*
Keel	*Coil*
Pick-thank	*Parasite*
Scuth	*Whip*
Slough	*Skin of a snake*

and the following Shakespearian words are also found in Lancashire folk-speech:

Antic	*Odd*
Ban	*Curse*
Bodge	*Repair clumsily*
Case	*Skin*
Gawd	*Trifle*
Hugger-mugger	*Slovenly*
Jump	*Agree*
Latch	*Take hold of*
Lob	*Dullard*
Paddock	*Toad*
Pash	*To strike*
Reechy	*Smoky*
Shive	*Slice*
Sneap	*Chide*
Thrum	*Waste end of a warp*
Whittle	*A small knife*

G.M.B.

THE ANNOTATOR
WHAT ABOUT THIS?

One more Lancashire echo, a somewhat cracked but picturesque one. In Leicester on a 'buying tour', I was searching for rarities among the shelves of mixed books in Backus's shop, when my wife pulled out an odd volume of Black's *Lancashire Stories* and called across 'What about this?' She had opened the popular pre-1914 miscellany on page 334 just where a pen-drawing of the Droeshout portrait of Shakespeare caught her eye, below the challenging title of the article in bold black type, DID SHAKESPEARE ACT IN LANCASHIRE? I promptly bought the odd volume, for in spite of its 'popular' character, the material of the article had some erudition to commend it, and now I think it interesting enough to quote in full, though of course to my mind Shakespeare was very much more likely to have been with Strange's men than with the Queen's during the years in question.

A.K.

DID SHAKESPEARE ACT IN LANCASHIRE?

This very interesting point is raised in a letter written by Mr E. J. L. Scott to the *Athenaeum* in January 1882. He quotes a letter from Henry le Scrope, ninth Baron Scrope of Bolton, Governor of Carlisle, and Warden of the West Marches, to the English Ambassador, William Asheby, at the Court of King James VI of Scotland, from which it appears that King James had desired to witness the performance of the Queen's Players, as the actors in the service of his cousin, Queen Elizabeth, were

APPENDIX IX

called. It is known that Shakespeare was a member of this company. Thus runs Lord Scrope's letter, with its old-world spelling:

> After my verie hertie comendacions: upon a letter receyved from Mr Roger Asheton, signifying unto me that yt was the kinges earnest desire for to have her Majesties players for to repayer into Scotland to his grace: I dyd furthwith dispatche a servant of my owen vnto them wheir they were in the furthest parte of Langkeshire, wherevpon they made their returne heather to Carliell, wher they are, and have stayed for the space of ten dayes, whereof I thought good to gyve yow notice in respect of the great desyre that the kynge had to have the same come vnto his grace; And withall to pray yow to gyve knowledg thereof to his Majestie. So for the present I bydd yow right hartelie farewell. Carlisle the XXth of September, 1589.
> Your verie assured loving frend,
> H. SCROPE.

Mr Scott says:

There is no further letter relating to the subject among Asheby's correspondence, but it is very interesting to think that Shakespeare visited Edinburgh at the very time when the witches were tried and burned for raising the storms that drowned Jane Kennedy, mistress of the robes to the new Queen, and imperilled the life of Anne of Denmark herself. In that case the witches in *Macbeth* must have had their origin from the actual scenes witnessed by the player so many years previously to the writing of that drama in 1606.

THE ANNOTATOR

The *Manchester City News* in reprinting this letter in February 1882, says:

> The letter is, however, specially worthy of note in these columns, because it shews not only that Shakespeare was in Edinburgh at the period named (1589), but that he and his company of players were summoned to go from Lancashire – here spelt 'Langkeshire'.

The Queen's Players were not kept for the exclusive pleasure of Queen Elizabeth, but during the absence of the Court made tours throughout the country. Thus they were at Stratford-on-Avon in 1587, the date upon which Shakespeare is supposed to have joined them. The Queen's Players were at Lathom House, giving performances before the Lord Derby of that time on 10 October 1588, and again at Knowsley in June 1590. This evidence would point to a two years' tour by the Players in the north, and to two visits to Lancashire, one before, and one after the command visit to Edinburgh, which would give Shakespeare a considerable knowledge of the country.

The warm interest taken both by King James and his Queen, Anne of Denmark, in Shakespeare and his plays after they became King and Queen of England, might reasonably be taken to have been founded on their former acquaintance with him at Edinburgh, and if Shakespeare was amongst the Queen's Players commanded to Edinburgh, then he must have acted in Lancashire, for it is proved beyond all doubt that the company of players summoned by King James, through the English Ambassador, went to Scotland directly from Lancashire.

X

The Newport Copy of Halle's *Chronicle*

PHYSICAL DESCRIPTION

HALLE, or HALL (Edward) THE UNI=on of the two noble and illustr(at)e fa= / melies of Lancastre & Yorke, beyng long / in continuall discension for the crowne of / this noble realme, with al the actes done / in both the tymes of the Princes, both of / the one linage & of the other, beginnyng / at the tyme of Kyng Henry the fowerth, / the first aucthor of this deuision, and so / successiuely proceadi(n)g to ye reigne of the / high and prudent Prince Kyng Henry / the eyght, the indubitate flower / and very heire of both the saied / linages. Whereunto is added / to euery kyng a / seuerall ta=ble. / 1550.

(*colophon*) Imprynted at London by / Rychard Grafton, Prynter to the Kynges Maiestye, / 1550. / *Cum priuilegio ad imprimendum solum.*

(*Hazlitt states that the* 1550 *edition was in fact printed for Grafton by Richard Jugge.*)

FOURTH ISSUE. Small thick folio, rebound in the late seventeenth or early eighteenth century: the binder in shortening the copy has cropped the margins, cutting into the MS. annotations. Lacks title-page and preliminaries, beginning on fol. i, and three leaves at the end of Table to *Henry VIII*. Fol. ii is also lacking and has been supplied in neat MS. by an early nineteenth century owner.

The title-page woodcut contained a pictorial 'tree'; fol. ii, *recto*, deals at length with the characters and often involved pedigrees of the Red and White Rose factions; and *verso* with the opening of the quarrel between Bolingbroke, afterwards Henry IV, and Mowbray, Duke of Norfolk. (*This title-page with its woodcuts is a distinguishing feature of the* 1550 *edition.*)

The nineteenth century owner has also pencilled in on the upper cover details of the missing leaves, and has marked the book throughout with crosses and underscoring in pencil, denoting doubtful or obsolete words. The eighteenth century owner, who apparently had the volume rebound in half-calf and marbled boards, affixed a library press-mark within the upper cover: a printed label **EEd**. A similar label, bearing a different alphabetical combination, **App.**, has been found in a folio copy of *The Theory of the Earth*, 1691, among the collections of Mr C. K. Ogden, now in the Library of University College, London. This book bears the signature of *Robert Worsley*, a descendant of Robert Worsley of Booths Esq., who visited Knowsley in 1587.

Three other people have marked the book: *Rychard Newport* (Sir Richard Newport, of High Ercall, Shropshire), perhaps the first owner, who has written his name twice, also his initials *R.N.* with the date '6. *Aprill ao.* 1565'. Then the name

APPENDIX X

'*Edward*' (apparently an Elizabethan schoolboy or child), once in ink and once pricked out with a pin. Finally, there are four hundred and six marginal notes with no indication of authorship. This annotator has also drawn one pointing finger, seventeen crosses, twelve marginal lines and underlinings.

He has also made one 'doodle', which might be taken to represent a man's head. This is found against the passage in *Henry V* recounting the episode of the 'foolishe souldier', which gave Shakespeare his idea for the death of Bardolph on the field of Agincourt. (H.v.f.xv.) The doodle was some time ago submitted to the scrutiny of Mr Augustus John, O.M., who commented 'decidedly a genuine sketch of a face and a good characterisation. The subject has lost his teeth so that, as happens in such cases, his lips blow at his nose.'

(*One Bardolph, if your majesty knows the man: his face is all bubulkes, and whelkes . . . and his lips blow at his nose.*)

These marginalia begin at fol. i and end abruptly at the fourth part of the *Chronicle, Henry VI*, on fol. ii *recto*, amounting to about three thousand six hundred words.

It has been found necessary to replace the old and perished calf of the spine of the book. This was expertly done in April 1951 by Mr C. E. Smart, who before rebacking the book in calf, antique style, resewed the gatherings, thus preserving the copy against further decay.

INDEX

Abington Hall, 200
Acheson, Arthur, *Shakespeare's Lost Years in London*, 58
Alexander, Professor Peter, 83
Allen, Cardinal William, 87, 96
Alleyn, Edward, 39, 42, 51-2, 57, 80
— Mrs (Edward), 51
Alty, Lawrence, 50
Arden, Edward, 104, 118
— Mary, 112-13, 118
— Robert, 112, 115
Ashcroft, Philip, 49
Asheton, Alice, 121
Aspinall, Alexander, 121, 122, 195-8

Baker, Oliver, *Shakespeare's Warwickshire and the Unknown Years*, 34, 42, 47, quoted 43-4, 74-5
Bampfield, Eleanor, 122
Barnard, E. A. B., *New Links with Shakespeare*, quoted 119
Barnard, John, 200
Beeston, Christopher, 42, 57
Bibliographical Dictionary of English Catholics, quoted 96-8
Black, *Lancashire Stories*, 206
Blackfriars Theatre, 37
Blanch, W. H., 51
Blount, Joyce, 119
Bradshaigh, James, 97
Brasenose College, 122, 187
Bromley, Margaret, 31
Brown, Geoffrey, 49
Buc, Sir George, 61
Burbage, Richard, 39, 42
Burleigh, William Cecil, Lord, 80
Bushell, Sir Edward, 117

Carey, George. *See* Hunsdon, Lord
— Henry, 41
Carill, Euphemia, 54
Cecil, Sir Robert, 62
Chaloner, Jacob, 32, 109
— Thomas, 33, 70
Chamberlain's Company, Lord, 41, 51, 64, 78
Chambers, Sir Edmund, 34, 37, 40, 50, 62, 84, 104n, 187; *Shakespearian Gleanings*, quoted 47, *William Shakespeare*, 168n
Chapman, George, *The Shadow of Night*, 56-8
Chester, Robert, *Love's Martyr*, 72 Mysteries, 180
Chetham Society, 47
Chettle, Henry, 110-11; *Kind-Harts Dreame*, quoted 111
Cobham, Henry Brooke, Lord, 62
Condell, Henry, 42, 119
Connes, Professor George, *The Shakespeare Mystery*, 56-8, 87
Corbet family, 114-16
Cottam, John, 102, 198
— Thomas, 102

Daston, Anne, 118
— Antony, 118
Davies, Rev. Richard, 99
Derby, Henry Stanley, fourth Earl of (1531-1593), 39, 41, 70, 81, 87, 202, 208
— Ferdinando Stanley, fifth Earl of, *see* Strange, Lord
— William Stanley, sixth Earl of (1561-1642), 56-9, 87

INDEX

Derby Household Books, 72, 93, 187, 190
Derby's Company, Lord, 39, 41
Dibdale, Robert, 101-3
Digges, Leonard, 123
Doleman, 87
Douay, 96-8, 102, 103
Drinkwater, Rev. C. H., *Transactions of Shropshire Archaeological Society*, 91*n*
Droeshout portrait, 199
Dugdale, Sir William, *Visitation of Shropshire*, 202
Dulwich College, 51
Durham Abbey, 35
Dyce, Alexander, 111

Easton Neston, 46, 200-1
Englefield, Father, 87
Essex, Robert Devereux, Earl of, 62, 114

Faire Em, 193
Fane, Sir Francis, 195
Farington, William, 47, 61, 72, 73, 186-94
First Folio, 42, 118, 123
Fitton family, 116-18
   Mary ('Dark Lady'), 33, 61, 116, 117
Fitzwater, Robert Radcliffe, second Lord, 62
Folger Shakespeare Library, 118
Folk Museum, Rufford Hall, 49
France, Sharpe, 53, 75
Freeman, Barbara, *Open to View*, quoted 45-6
Fripp, Edgar I., *Shakespeare Man and Artist*, quoted 88-90, 102, 104*n*, 195, 196
Fuller, Thomas, *Worthies*, 52

Gerard, Catherine, 94
   Elizabeth, 94
   Sir Gilbert, 121
   Katherine, 121
   Sir Thomas, 94, 96

Globe Theatre, 33, 37, 50, 116
Gollancz, Sir Israel, *A Book of Homage to Shakespeare*, 187
Grafton, Richard, 8, 22, 209
Grafton portrait, the, 199-201
Greene, Robert, 35, 47, 75, 81-2, 83, 107, 110; *Menaphon*, 79, 81; *The Myrrour of Modestie*, 81; *Ciceronis Amor*, 81; *Groatsworth of Wit*, 82, 111
Grosart, Rev. Alexander, *The Towneley MSS.*, 197
Gyllome, Foke, 35, 44, 46

Hall, John, 200
Halle, Edward, 8-19
Halliday, Dick, 32
Halliday, F. E., *Shakespeare Companion*, quoted 63, 64-5
Halliwell-Phillipps, J. O., 202, 203
Harrison, Professor, *Shakespeare's Fellows*, 41
Harsnett, Samuel, *Declaration of Egregious Popish Imposters*, 101
Hathaway, Anne, 79, 102
Hazlitt, W. Carew, *Shakespeare, the Man and his Work*, quoted, 54-5; 209
Heard, Sir Isaac, 202
Heminges, John, 33, 42, 50, 119, 193
Henslowe, Philip, 63, 64, 65
Henty, William, *Shakespeare. With some Notes on his Early Biography*, quoted 111-12
Herbert, A. J., 66
Herbert, George, 32, 115
   Sir Henry, 115
   Richard, 31, 115
   of Cherbury, Lord, 31-2
Hesketh, Elizabeth, 121
   Lord, 46, 201
   Margaret, 121
   Sir Thomas, 34, 36, 44-7, 51, 52, 80, 81, 93, 117, 194, 196, 201

INDEX

Hesketh's Players, Sir Thomas, 39, 72, 194
Holcroft, Captain, 73
Holcroft, Hamlet, 73
  Margaret, 121
  Sir Thomas, 52, 118
Holinshed, Raphael, 8-9, 14, 22, 84, 164-87 *passim.*
Holme, Randle, 33
Hotson, Professor Leslie, 33; *Shakespeare's Sonnets Dated,* 50, 51, 61-2, *I, William Shakespeare,* 122
Houghton, Alexander (1), 34, 43, 44, 47, 77, 94, 121, 198
  Alexander (2), 121
  Elizabeth, 77
  John, 121
  Richard, 97, 103
  Sir Richard (1), 44, 121
  Sir Richard (2), 52, 121
  Thomas (1), 77, 94, 96-8, 103, 121
  Thomas (2), 34, 44, 47, 96, 121
  Thomas (3), 97-8
Huband, Ralph, 118-19
Hunsdon, George Carey, Lord, 41, 56, 58
Hunt, Simon, 96, 102

James I, King, 41
Jerusalem, 64
John, Mr Augustus, O.M., 211
Jonson, Ben, 61, 123
Jugge, Richard, 209

Kay, Thomas, 199; *Story of the Grafton Portrait,* 200n
Killing the Calf, 77-9
King's Men, 41
Knack to Know a Knave, A, 64-5
Knowsley, 39, 53, 61, 66, 72, 81, 82, 85, 106, 188, 192, 202, 208
Kyd, Thomas, 63

Lacon, Beatrix, 115
  Thomas, 114

Lady Isabella's Tragedy (ballad), quoted 67-8
Lathom House, 39, 57, 70, 86, 190, 202, 208
Lea Old Hall, 34, 43, 46, 79, 97, 103, 106, 198
Lefranc, Professor Abel, 59
Leicester, Robert Dudley, Earl of, 39, 41, 57
Leicester's Company, Earl of, 39, 40, 41, 57, 60, 193
Leveson, Elizabeth, 118
  Sir John, 115, 116
  Sir Richard (1, 2 and 3), 116
  William, 33, 51
Lloyd, Richard, 57-60
Long-Brown, Norman, 109-10
Longworth de Chambrun, Clara, *Shakespeare Rediscovered,* quoted 98-9
Lucy, Sir Thomas, 114
Ludgate family, 199

McLaren, Moray, 13
Manchester City News, 208
Marlowe, Christopher, 63
Martholme Manor, 45, 196
Mitton, Edward, 115
  Richard, 115-16, 117
Monteagle, Lord, 117
More, Sir Thomas, 7, 105, 165, 166
Morley, Alice, 121

Nash, Elizabeth, 204
  John, 119, 204
  John, of Martley, 204
  Thomas (1), 119; (2), 200
Nashe, Thomas, 79, 107; *Pierce Pennilesse,* quoted 83n
Neill, Miss Diana, 95
New Place, 5, 39, 197, 203
Newport, Sir Francis, 115
  John, 120
  Magdalen, 115
  Richard, 5, 31
  Sir Richard, 31-4, 94, 115, 124, 210
  Thomas, 115

INDEX

Nicoll, Professor, 171
Nine Worthies, The, 59-60
Northumberland, Henry Percy, ninth Earl of, 56-8
Nosworthy, J. M., 52
Nowell, Grace, 121
— Robert, 36, 122, 197

O'Donnell, Elliott, *Haunted Britain*, 67
Ogden, C. K., 91-2, 210
Oldys, Cecilia, 119-20
— Rev. Thomas, 120
— William, 120

Parsons, Robert, 87
Peele, George, 64, 174n; *Honour of the Garter*, quoted 58
Percy, Sir Charles, 116-17
Piccope, Rev. G. J., *Lancashire and Cheshire Wills*, 47
Plenderleith, Dr, 3-4
Pollard, A. W., *Shakespeare's Hand in the Play of Sir Thomas More*, 105, 165n
Prescot playhouse, 53-4, 84

Queen's Players, 40, 208
Quiney, Richard, 115, 117

Radcliffe, Margaret, 61 62
— Sir Alexander, 61, 62
— Tower, 67, 68
Raines, Canon, *Derby Household Books*, 45, 47, 72, 93; quoted 187-9
Ratseis Ghost, 38
Read Hall, 36, 196
Rhodes, H. T. F., 7, 105
Roche, Walter, 106
Rose Theatre, 64, 107
Rufford Hall, 43, 45, 46, 49, 60, 80, 81, 82, 106, 194, 198
Russell, Thomas, 118, 122-3
Rylands Library, Manchester, 199

Salisbury, Sir John, 72

Sandells, Fulke, 102
Savage family, 118-20
— Thomas, 50, 51, 116, 120
'School of Night' allusion, 56-60
Scott, E. J. L., 206, 207
Severne family, 203-4
Shakeshafte, William, 35, 40, 43-7, 50, 51, 60, 72, 75, 103, 197
Shakespeare, John, 75-8, 81, 85, 104, 113
— Richard, 75
— Susannah, 79, 200
— William (plays and poems):
  All's Well that Ends Well, 100
  Comedy of Errors, 28
  Cymbeline, 100-1
  Hamlet, 73, 78
  Henry IV, Part II, 18-19, 27, 28
  Henry V, 1, 15, 22-6, 29, 211
  Henry VI, Part I, 15, 25, 28, 82-3, 107, 108, 167, 168n
  Henry VI, Part II, 83, 84
  Henry VI, Part III, 83, 84
  King John, 66, 171-2, 174, 183, 184n
  King Lear, 101
  Love's Labour's Lost, 22, 54-60, 99
  Lucrece, 82
  Phoenix and Turtle, 72
  Richard II, 24, 27, 53, 114, 117, 170, 172, 180, 181
  Richard III, 18, 53, 84, 173n
  Taming of the Shrew, 22, 98
  Titus Andronicus, 63-71
  Twelfth Night, 29, 196
  Venus and Adonis, 82
Shakespeare Association Bulletin, 186
Shaw, Ann, 121-2, 195-6
— Julius, 195
Sheldon family, 118
Smart, John Semple, *Shakespeare Truth and Tradition*, 76, 199
Southampton, Henry Wriothesley, third Earl of, 82, 114
Stanley, Sir Edward, 202-3

215

INDEX

Stanley, Sir Thomas, 202-3
  Ursula, 72
  family, 83-7, 186-94, 202-3; *see also* Derby, Earls of; Strange, Lord
Steevens, George, 64, 65
Stopes, Charlotte Carmichael, 122; *Shakespeare's Warwickshire Contemporaries*, 196
Strange, Ferdinando, Lord (later fifth Earl of Derby, 1559-1594), 39, 41, 86
Strange's Company, Lord, 39, 40-1, 51, 54, 64-6, 81, 83, 84, 107, 190, 192, 193
Stratford Grammar School, 96, 195
Surtees Society, Transactions of, 35
Sussex, Thomas Radcliffe, third Earl of (1526?-1583), 63
Sussex's Company, Earl of, 63-4, 68

Tannenbaum, *The Booke of Sir Thomas More*, 154
Thaler, Professor Alwin, *Faire Em in Lancashire*, 80n, 189n; 'The Original Malvolio', 186-94
Theory of the Earth, The, 92, 210
Throckmorton, Anne, 118
Titherley, Dr A. W., 59
Titus and Vespasian (play), 65, 66
Titus and Vespasian, or the Destruction of Jerusalem (poem), 66

Tofte, Robert, 54-5, 61; *Alba*, quoted 54
Towneley, Margaret, 51
Trafford, Sir Edmund, 80, 98, 194

Underhill family, 5

Vernon, Elizabeth, 61, 62, 114
  Sir John, 114

Weever, John, 55; *Epigrammes*, 52, 53; *Faunus and Melliflora*, 52
Williams, Sara, 101
Willoughby, Henry, *Willobie his Avisa*, 122
Wilson, Professor Dover, 8, 23, 56, 63, 64, 65, 71, 82, 107, 170, 171, 172, 174, 179, 180, 183n, 199; *The Essential Shakespeare*, 199, quoted 76-7; preface to *Henry VI, Part I*, quoted 83
Worcester's Company, Earl of, 80
Worsley, Robert (1), 80, 92-4, 98
  Robert (2), 92, 210

Yates, Dr Francis, *A Study of Love's Labour's Lost*, 56

Zeeveld, Dr Gordon, *The Influence of Halle on Shakespeare's Historical Plays*, 9, 21

CHART 1

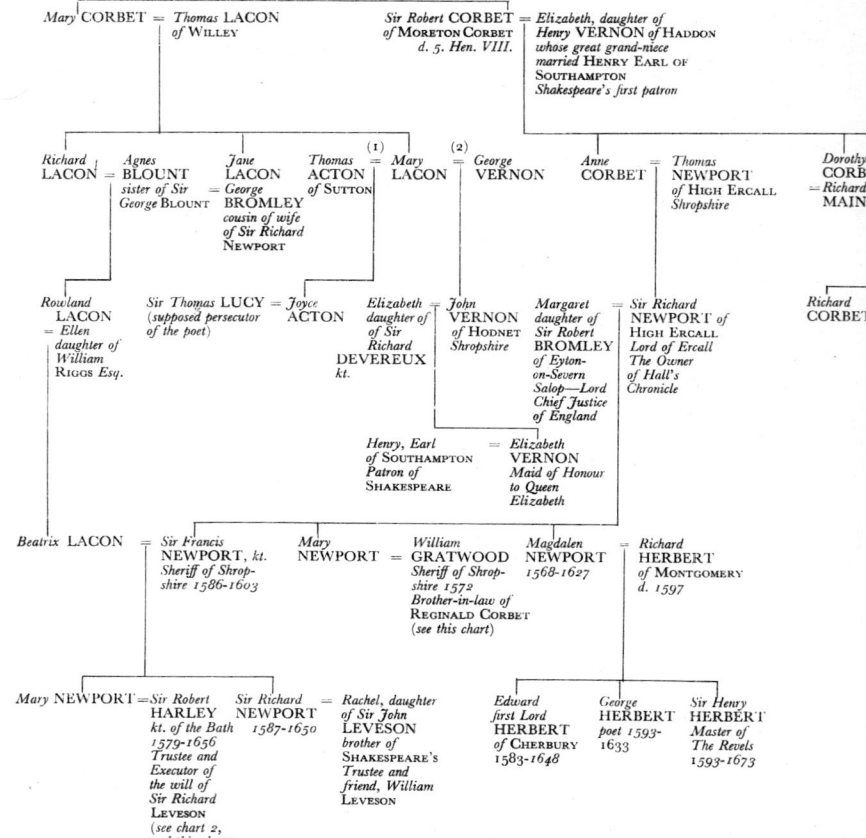

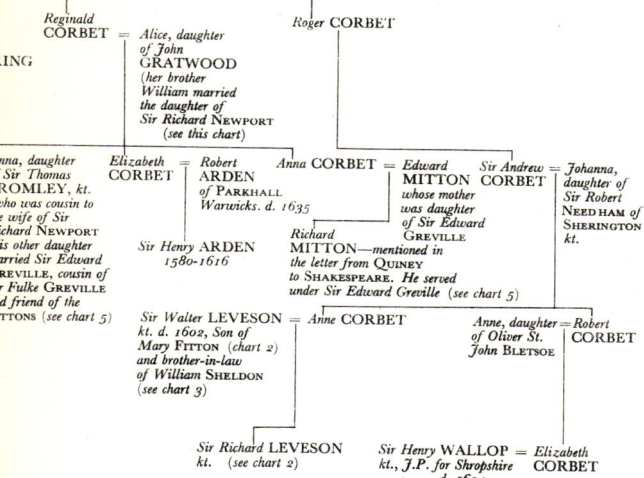

CHART 2

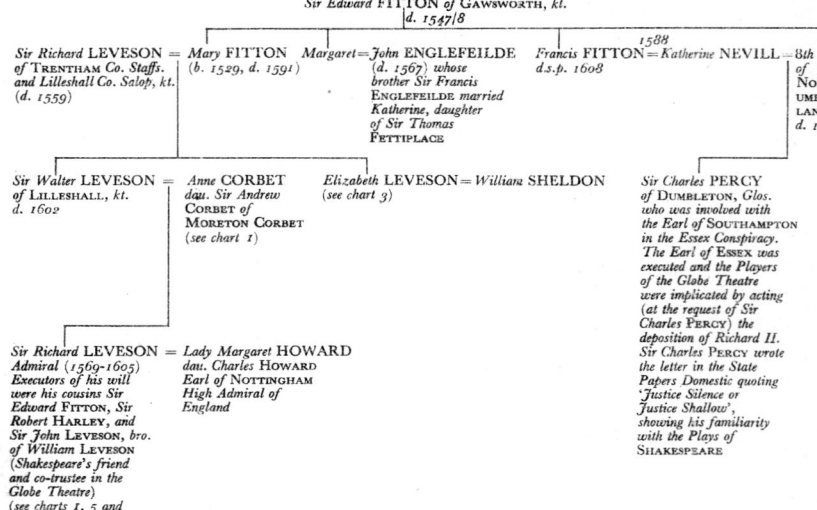

                              Sir Edward FITTON of GAWSWORTH, kt.
                                         d. 1547/8
       ┌─────────────────┬──────────────┬──────────────────────┬───────────────────────────────┐
                                                                      1588
Sir Richard LEVESON = Mary FITTON   Margaret = John ENGLEFEILDE   Francis FITTON = Katherine NEVILL — 8th Earl
of TRENTHAM Co. Staffs. (b. 1529, d. 1591)   (d. 1567) whose   d.s.p. 1608   of
and Lilleshall Co. Salop, kt.   brother Sir Francis   NORTH-
(d. 1559)   ENGLEFEILDE married   UMBER-
                                                   Katherine, daughter   LAND
                                                   of Sir Thomas   d. 1585
                                                   FETTIPLACE

┌──────────────────────┬──────────────────────┬────────────────────────────────┐
Sir Walter LEVESON = Anne CORBET   Elizabeth LEVESON = William SHELDON   Sir Charles PERCY
of LILLESHALL, kt.   dau. Sir Andrew   (see chart 3)   of DUMBLETON, Glos.
d. 1602   CORBET of   who was involved with
                      MORETON CORBET   the Earl of SOUTHAMPTON
                      (see chart 1)   in the Essex Conspiracy.
                                                                                       The Earl of ESSEX was
                                                                                       executed and the Players
                                                                                       of the Globe Theatre
                                                                                       were implicated by acting
                                                                                       (at the request of Sir
                                                                                       Charles PERCY) the
                                                                                       deposition of Richard II.
Sir Richard LEVESON = Lady Margaret HOWARD   Sir Charles PERCY wrote
Admiral (1569-1605)   dau. Charles HOWARD   the letter in the State
Executors of his will Earl of NOTTINGHAM   Papers Domestic quoting
were his cousins Sir High Admiral of   'Justice Silence or
Edward FITTON, Sir   England   Justice Shallow',
Robert HARLEY, and   showing his familiarity
Sir John LEVESON, bro.   with the Plays of
of William LEVESON   SHAKESPEARE
(Shakespeare's friend
and co-trustee in the
Globe Theatre)
(see charts 1, 5 and
this chart)

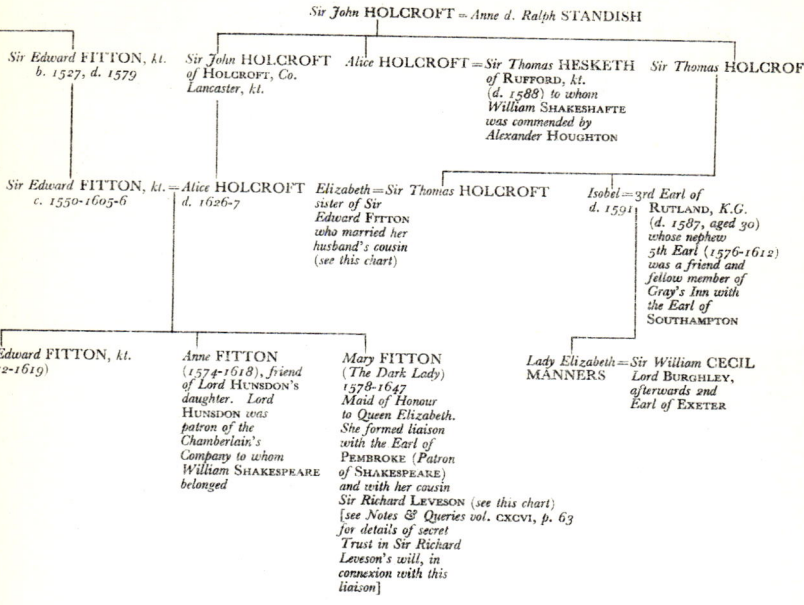

CHART 3

Mary WILLINGTON = William SHELDON (*founder of*
grand-daughter of Sir   *the Tapestry looms on his estates*
Robert THROCKMORTON   *in Worcestershire and Warwickshire*)

| Elizabeth LEVESON dau. Mary FITTON (see chart 2) | William SHELDON | Ralph SHELDON | = | Anne THROCKMORTON *sister-in-law to Edward* ARDEN *who was a kinsman of* SHAKESPEARE'S *mother (see chart 5)* | Katherine SHELDON | = | Edmund PLOWDEN (d. 1585) *of the Middle Temple; the greatest lawyer of his age—a strong Romanist* |

| Richard LYGON *of* MADRESFIELD | Mary = RUSSELL | Sir John RUSSELL *half-brother of Thomas* RUSSELL *(1570-1634) overseer of the will of* SHAKESPEARE *(see chart 5)* | = | Elizabeth SHELDON | Edward SHELDON | Anne DASTON | = | 1584 Ralph HUBAND *from whom* SHAKESPEARE *bought the tithes in 1605. He was the cousin of Thomas* NASH *whose sons* ANTHONY *and* JOHN *were legatees of* SHAKESPEARE |

Eleanor LYGON = John WASHBOURNE
b. 1548, d. 1633/4
whose grandson
William WASHBOURNE
entered into sale of
land to Henry CONDELL
SHAKESPEARE'S *friend*
and co-actor

William SHELDON
owner of the 1st Folio
of SHAKESPEARE'S PLAYS
(*Burdett Coutts copy*)
now in the FOLGER
LIBRARY

† *These people were all parties to the transactions with Henry* CONDELL *and the* WASHBOURNE *family in 1617 and 1619*

* *In 1587 Anthony* NASH *witnessed a document between four of these parties conveying land to Richard* LANE *who in 1596/7 witnessed the deed of sale by John* SHAKE-SPEARE *of property in Stratford-on-Avon. With* SHAKESPEARE *and Thomas* GREENE *he complained in 1609 to the Lord Chancellor about the Stratford-on-Avon Tithes.*
In 1591 a document between all these parties * *was witnessed by Richard* DASTON, *Richard* SAVAGE, *Edmund* WHITE, *Henry* BRANDON, *Wm.* RAM-SAYE *and* "W.S."

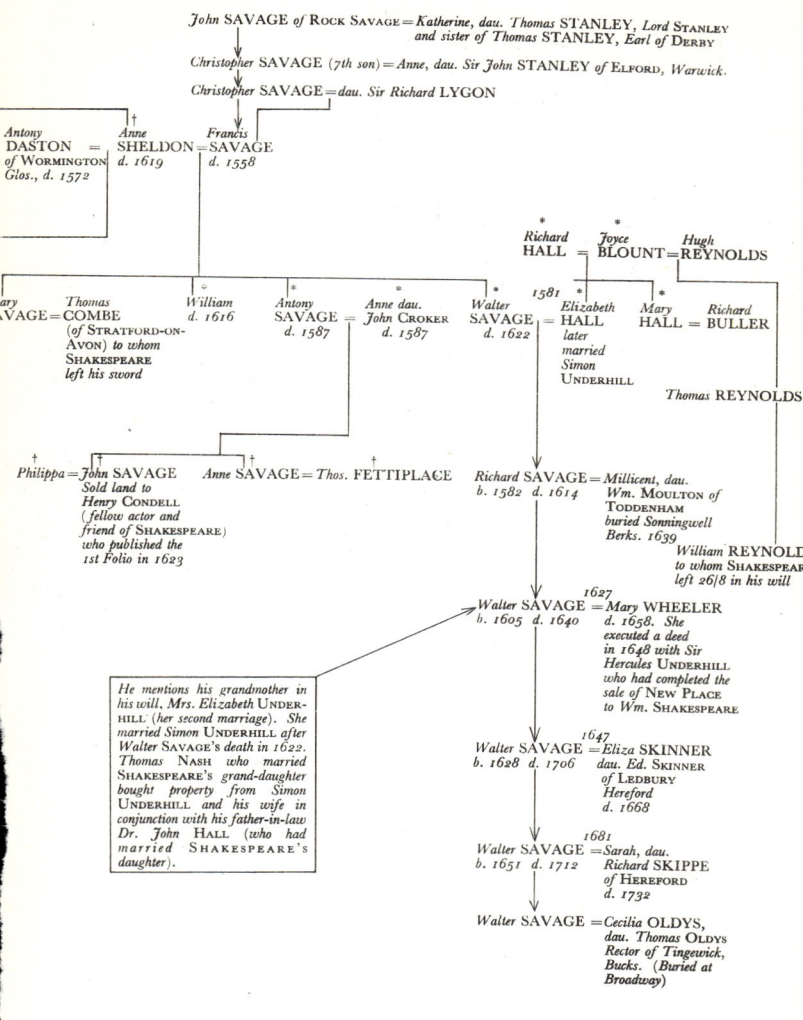

CHART 4

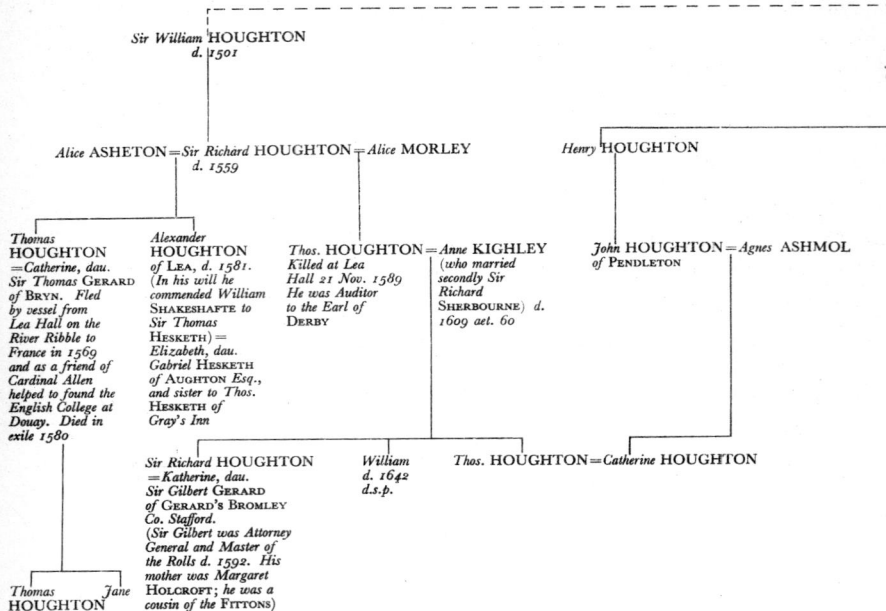

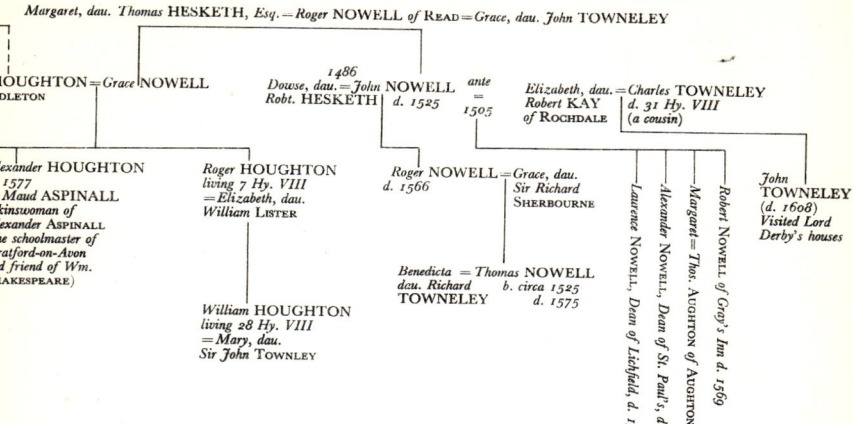

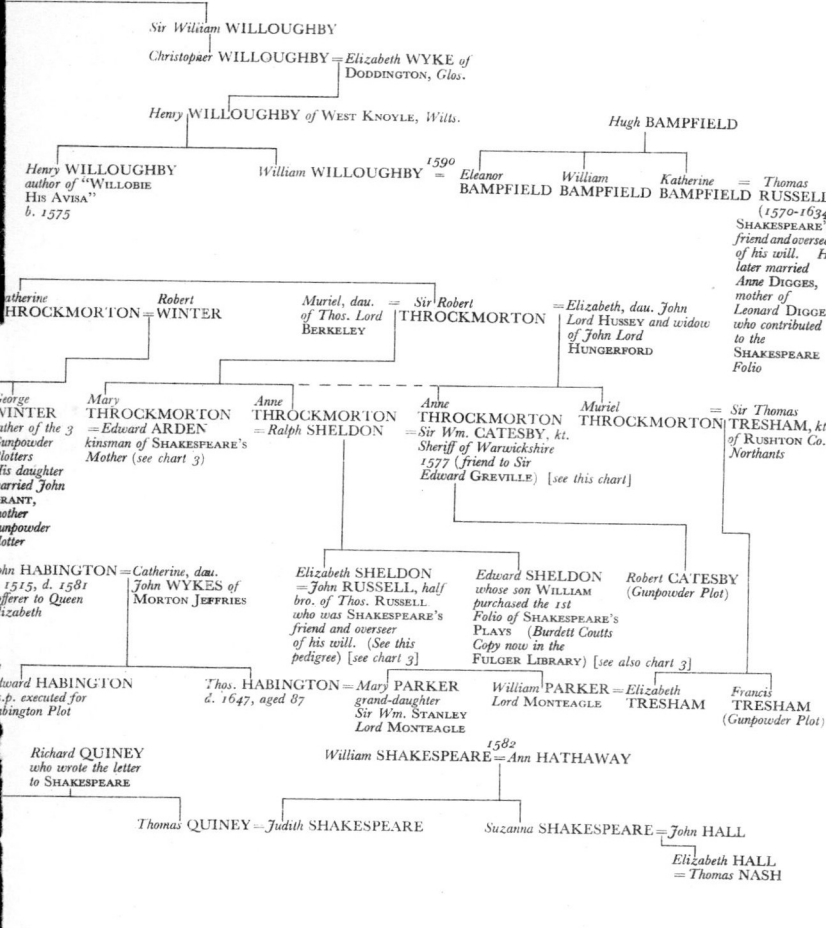

CHART 5

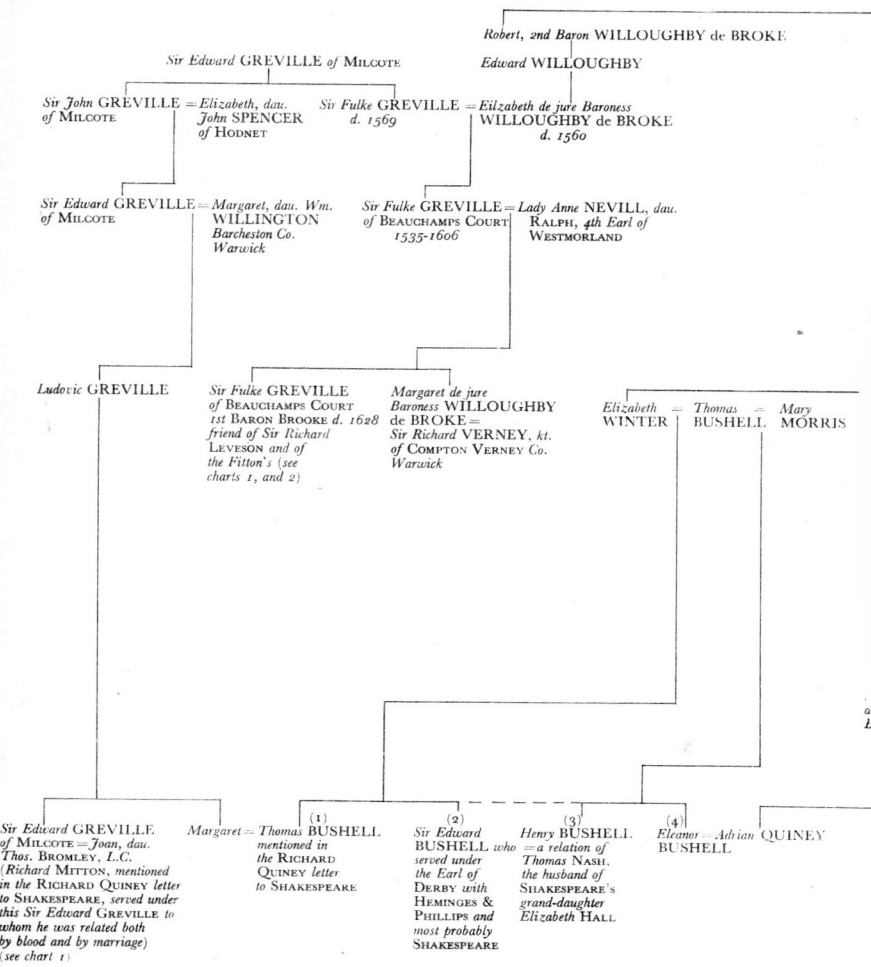